Lower Michigan's Best 75 Campgrounds

Other Books By Jim DuFresne:

Michigan State Parks

Michigan: Off The Beaten Path

Wild Michigan

Michigan's Best Outdoor Adventures With Children

50 Hikes In Lower Michigan

Porcupine Mountains Wilderness State Park

Isle Royale National Park

LOWER MICHIGAN'S BEST

75

CAMPGROUNDS

By Jim DuFresne

Production and design by Pegg Legg Publications

Published by Thunder Bay Press

1-882376-18-8

Printed in the United States of America

10 9 8 7 6 5 4 3 2   99 98 97 96

CONTENTS

RUSTIC CABINS

THE TIP

NORTH-WEST

LAKE HURON

LAKE MICHIGAN

SOUTH-EAST

HEARTLAND

The beach access at Lake Michigan Recreation Area in the Manistee National Forest.

WHY CAMP?

Why camp? Why not?

It's affordable and nearby. It's lodging on the lake, great scenery from your front door, a 9-inch bluegill at the end of your line. It's fresh air, towering pines, a crackling fire on a starry night. It's an air mattress in a two-man tent or a waterbed in a recreational vehicle complete with a microwave oven, television and an ice-maker in the freezer.

Camping is anything you want it to be. The purpose of this guide is not to tell you how to camp, there are many other books that will do that, but where to go. And in Michigan there are many places to go. Across the state there are approximately 1,280 campgrounds with 92,803 designated sites on public and private land. Within the Michigan State Park System alone there are 14,500 sites, more than other state park system in the country. Add another 1,680 sites in the three national forests, 3,200 sites in the state forests and countless more in country parks and private campgrounds and you can see the need for a guide.

To narrow it down, this Glovebox Guidebook covers only the Lower Peninsula and has chosen the best 75 public campgrounds and cabins. It's been my experience that the very nature of public land allows those campsites to be located along lakes, rivers or the Great Lakes and have the acreage to provide opportunities for hiking, swimming, boating and other traditional activities of the summer camping season.

For the purpose of easy reference the state has been divided into five regions; Southeast, Heartland, Lake Michigan, Lake Huron, Northwest and The Tip. The book has also been divided into three types of campsites:

Modern: Although modern campgrounds vary widely, all of these have at least electrical hook-ups at each site and a modern restroom with showers. When the facility also provides on-site spigots, sanitation stations for trailers or other amenities it has been clearly noted. Keep in mind that the high cost of equipping sites with electricity forces most parks to keep them relatively close together. For the want of an outlet, you sacrifice solitude.

Rustic: These campgrounds lack hook-ups and for the most part modern restrooms and showers unless noted. Vault toilets (also known as pit toilets, outhouses and "the shack") are a way of life in rustic campgrounds. Also noted in each one is the terrain, forest and ground cover. A rustic campground whose sites are well spread out in a thick forest with good underbrush is going to provide privacy between campers and a feeling that you're actually spending a night in the woods.

Cabins: Within the state park system there are more than 85 rustic cabins for rent. These are ideal for families and groups who don't have access to a recreational vehicle but want something more comfortable than a tent for a weekend outdoors. Cabins come with bunks, mattresses, tables and chairs, but also have vault toilets and hand pumps for water outside. The ones chosen for this guide are the best for scenery, solitude and the water resources they are near.

Reservations and Seasons

Information on fees, reservations, amenities, and season of operation is given as well as a description of the campground and the area. Reservations allow you to secure a site in advance so when you arrive late Friday evening you're guaranteed a spot for your trailer. Most modern campgrounds offer this service, but not all, and a handful of rustic facilities also offer advanced reservations.

In 1992, all Michigan state parks began accepting campsite payments with a Visa and Mastercard credit card and in 1993, the Parks Division will switch over to a centralized reservation system. By employing a 1-800-number, you will be able to reserve a site in any Michigan state park with a single call. Call the state's Park Division at (517) 373-1270 for the latest on the reservation phone number. Before then, and even afterwards, you can still reserve a site by contacting the individual parks.

Seasons of operation are also listed. Some campgrounds are literally locked during the off-season, others simple lack a host to collect fees. State forest campgrounds are technically open year-round though during the winter the roads may not be plowed and the handles may be removed from water pumps.

One last thing; in these deficit budget times, keep in mind that public facilities, policies and fees can change quickly. Some are small such as a $1 increase in a camping fee, some are quite significant such as the state's decision to close a number of state forest campgrounds. It's best to always call the information number provided to double check. One thing that will never change, however; a scenic little campground on the edge of a lake in the middle of the woods will always be a scenic little campground on the edge of a lake in the middle of the woods.

And that's the main reason why this guidebook should be in every camper's glovebox.

MODERN
CAMPGROUNDS

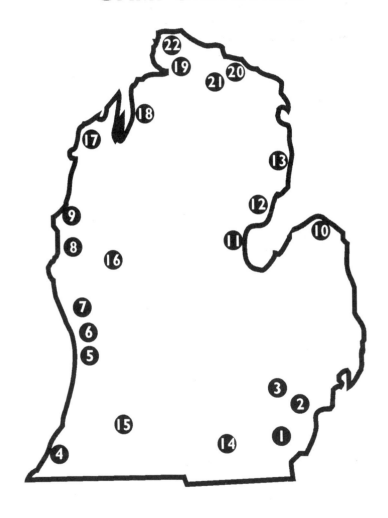

1

PROUD LAKE
STATE PARK

Region: Southeast
Nearest Community: Wixom
Sites: 130   **Reservations:** Yes
Fee: $13 plus vehicle entry fee
Information: Park headquarters (313) 685-2433

Wixom and the I-96 corridor in southwest Oakland County is a growing overload of shopping centers, strip malls, apartment complexes and other signs of a metropolitan Detroit area bursting at the seams. You pass through all this and just before reaching Proud Lake skirt an incredibly large trailer park.

Not the kind of setting most people envision for a camping trip but be patient. Once in the park it's like entering a different world. Proud Lake is a 3,727-acre recreation area whose rolling forested hills, wetlands and undeveloped stretch of the Huron River is the fortress against the uncontrolled growth of Oakland County. Next to Addison Oaks County Park (see page 14), Proud Lake is probably the most pleasant modern campground in Southeast Michigan.

Directions: The state recreation area is just east of Milford or 12 miles southwest of Pontiac. From I-96, depart at exit 159 and head north on Wixom Road. The road passes through the town of Wixom and then makes a 90-degree turn left. You head right onto Glengary Road and the campground entrance is less than a mile to the east.

Campground: The campground is in the east half of the park and totally separated from the day-use beach and canoe livery. It's a large loop of 130 modern sites in an open, grassy area on a bluff that overlooks a chain of lakes formed by the Huron River. These are scenic lakes as the opposite bank is an undeveloped shoreline of cattails and marshes.

Sites are open and close together as is typical of most state park modern campgrounds but most have a good view of the water below. Tables, fire rings and hookups are provided in each site while along the loop are two restroom buildings with showers, vault toilets and a sanitation station. The only drawback at Proud Lake is the major power line that runs across the west end of the lake and skirts the campground.

Day-Use Facilities: A staircase leads from the campground to an open grassy area along Proud Lake. No beach here but the swimming area is shallow with a bottom of soft sand. Nearby is limited playground equipment. The main swimming area for Proud Lake is Powers Beach, located off Wixom Road in the western half of the park. The small sandy beach and pond was made by impounding the Huron River while nearby are two picnic areas with tables and grills.

Fishing: An improved boat launch with a cement slab is located next to the swimming area but parking is back in the campground. Both Proud Lake and the Huron River is fished for panfish and smallmouth bass. The river within the park, from Moss Lake to Wixom Road, also has a special flies-only, catch-and-release trout season during April.

Hiking: A foot trail leads from the west end of the campground loop and connects with Marsh Trail and the rest of the park's 11-mile trail system. *Marsh Trail* is a 1.25-mile loop around a wetland area. Across the park road from the wetland loop is the winter ski center and the *Main Ski Loop*, a 2-mile trail that winds through a red pine plantation and hardwoods before heading back to the parking area.

Canoeing: A popular activity during the summer is paddling the Huron River and within the park is a canoe rental concession located off Garden Road on the opposite side of the river from Powers Beach. The *Heavner Canoe Center* (313-685-2379) is open 10 a.m. to 8 p.m. weekdays and from 9 a.m. to 9 p.m. weekends and holidays. You can either paddle up the river and then turn around or make arrangements with the concessionaire to be picked up down river.

Season: Proud Lake is open year-round and features heated restrooms during the winter. Because it's so close to metropolitan Detroit, the campground is heavily used on weekends from early May through mid-September.

2

ADDISON OAKS
OAKLAND COUNTY PARK

Region: Southeast
Nearest Community: Lake Orion
Sites: 93   **Reservations:** No
Fee: $9 to $17
Information: Park office (313) 693-2432

A trip to Addison Oaks County Park is a drive through the country; passing apple orchards, strawberry farms and fields where horse and cattle still graze. It's not the Northwoods but this 700-acre park offers a remarkable escape from the urban sprawl of this region of the state as well as some of the best campsites to be found anywhere in Southeast Michigan.

You won't find that deep-in-the-woods serenity that many state forest campgrounds up-north provide, but you will discover wooded sites, some even with electricity, and much to do here. Activities range from fishing and swimming to volleyball, renting a pedal boat even playing a round of disc golf.

Directions: From M-59 depart north on M-150 (Rochester Road) and follow it through downtown Rochester. The park is 9 miles north of Rochester and reached by turning west (left) on Romeo Road.

Campground: On the north side of Buhl Lake, but not on the water itself, is a modern campground and another labeled "primitive." The modern is a four-lane loop of 50 sites in an open grassy area bordered by woods. The sites include tables, fire rings with grills, cement slabs and hook-ups for water and electricity. There's a large restroom with showers within the loop while nearby is play equipment and a sanitation station.

The primitive campground is a loop with 42 sites that are well separated from each other on a wooded hillside of towering white and red pine and hardwoods. Add a thick undergrowth and you have some of the most secluded sites in southern Michigan. Sites 51-73 have electric outlets and are considered semi-modern, the rest are rustic. The loop is serviced by a pair of handicapped-access vault toilets and spigots for water. Tables and fire rings with grills are located at each site.

Day-use Facilities: Along the south side of Buhl Lake, less than half mile from the campgrounds is a large open day-use area that includes tables, pedestal grills, two shelters with one overlooking the lake, horseshoe pits, volleyball courts, considerable play equipment and an 18-hole disc golf course that is played with Frisbees.

Along Lake Adams, a spring-fed pond, is the park's swimming area. The facilities include a large sandy beach surrounded by a grassy slope, lifeguards, bathhouse and a concession building.

Boating: There is a unimproved launch on Buhl Lake next to the boat rental along with additional parking for vehicles and rigs. Boats are rented daily during the summer from 7 a.m. to sundown with pedal boats for $3 a half-hour and row boats $3 a half-hour or $10 a day.

Fishing: Buhl is heavily fished during the summer but attracts little attention after October. Prime species seems to be bluegill, pumpkinseed sunfish and black crappie. Anglers also catch an occasional largemouth bass and every year a few three and four-pound northern pike are landed. The boat rental station also sells limited bait.

Hiking: On its east side, the park maintains almost 4 miles of foot trails but most of them simply wind through the open day-use area or follow park roads back to the campground.

Mountain Biking: On the west side of park is a 5-mile network of trails designated for mountain bikers. *Buck Run Loop* winds through a hilly, wooded area and the rest pass through open fields where in the fall you can often see deer. In fact, the park is experiencing such an explosion in its deer population that officials are considering allowing bow hunting to reduce the herd.

Season: Camping begins from end of April or early May, depending on the weather, to mid-October. This is a popular campground and fills daily on a first-come-first-serve basis June through Labor Day. Oakland County residents pay $9 for a rustic site, $11 for semi-modern and $13 for the modern sites where you must have either a trailer, pop-up camper or a recreational vehicle to stay there. Non-residents pay $13 for rustic, $15 for semi-modern and $17 for a modern site. The park staff is exploring the possibility of reserving some sites in advance beginning in 1992.

3 METAMORA-HADLEY
STATE RECREATION AREA

Region: Southeast
Nearest Community: Hadley
Sites: 220   **Reservations:** Yes
Fee: $10 plus a vehicle entry permit
Information: Park headquarters (313) 797-4439

This would be a nice campground anywhere in the Lower Peninsula, for Southeast Michigan it's exceptional. Located in the southern half of Lapeer County, less than a half hour drive from Pontiac, Metamora-Hadley surrounds man-made Lake Minnawanna. The 683-acre state park unit features not only the lake and fishing opportunities but a nice beach, wooded trails and even shoreline sites. Yet the park draws only 220,000 visitors annually and most of them are day users.

This campground can accommodate you even if your family doesn't want to sleep in a tent. In 1991, Metamora-Hadley was one of three state parks that instituted a new mini-cabin program. The small cabins are located within the campground and sleep four but otherwise it's just like camping, where you would cook, eat and spend your day outside.

Directions: From I-75 depart at exit 81 and head north on M-24 through the towns of Lake Orion and Oxford. At Pratt Road, 20 miles north of the interstate, turn west (left) for 2 miles and then south (left) on Hurd Road to the park entrance.

Campground: Metamora-Hadley has 220 sites on two loops along the west side of the lake. The first loop reached has sites 128-220 in an open, grassy area shaded by a handful of towering pines and hardwoods. Twenty of them are right on the water, directly across from the park's day-use area. The second loop is far more scenic with sites 1-127 situated in a hilly area lightly forested in oaks and maples. Nine sites are on the edge of a shoreline bluff with a scenic view of the entire lake. Posted trailheads and the two mini-cabins are located here and both loops have sanitation stations, shower and restrooms, tables and fire rings at every site and limited playground equipment.

Day-use Facilities: At the north end of the lake is a wide beach and open, grassy picnic grounds. Facilities include bathhouse, tables, pedestal

A young hiker pauses on a foot bridge in Metamora-Hadley.

grills and a concession operator who rents rowboats, canoes and pedalboats. Along the east side of the lake in a pleasant wooded setting is another picnic area with a shelter.

Fishing: Lake Minnawanna, a 60-acre impoundment of the South Branch of Farmers Creek, features several species of fish but is best known by bass anglers. Anglers concentrate in the southern half of the lake and around a small island on the east side using standard bass baits and lures. Other species caught include bluegill, perch and an occasional northern pike.

There is an unimproved boat launch and dock at the north end of the lake with additional parking for a handful of vehicles. There are also three fishing piers along the west shore of the lake; at the boat launch and one at each campground loop.

Hiking: The park has a 6-mile network of trails that basically forms a loop from the campgrounds around the lake to the beach area on the east side. On the west side you wander from a marsh area to woods to open fields. On the east the path winds through a wooded area and an especially nice walk is to begin near the mini-cabins, cross the South Branch of Farmers Creek and then follow the loop around the picnic area, a round-trip hike of almost 2 miles.

Season: The campground is open April through October and reservations can be made by contacting the park headquarters. Despite being so close to metropolitan Detroit, Metamora-Hadley receives only moderate use on weekdays during the summer and sites are often available on non-holiday weekends.

WARREN DUNES
STATE PARK

Region: Lake Michigan
Nearest Community: Bridgman
Sites: 197   **Reservations:** Yes
Fee: $13 plus vehicle entry permit
Information: Park headquarters (616) 426-4013

Warren Dunes may be a Michigan state park but every summer it's invaded by Hoosiers and Chicagoians. The 1,507-acre unit is the first preserve along Lake Michigan and only 12 miles north of the state border. Thus of the 1.3 million visitors Warren Dunes draws every year, the second highest total in the park system, more than 80 percent of them are from outside of Michigan. For this reason Warren Dunes is the only park in the state that charges a higher entry fee for non-residents.

Still they pack this beautiful stretch of dunes and shoreline and the reason is clear. The park has 2.5-miles of undeveloped lakeshore, 200-foot high sand dunes that are a haven for hang gliders and a wooded campground that still provides a little space between parties. The trick here is getting a site and sometimes just getting inside the park.

Directions: Warren Dunes is reached from I-94 by departing at exit 16 and following Red Arrow Highway south to the park entrance.

Campground: Warren Dunes has 197 sites on two loops located away from the lake on the back side of the dunes. The loops are located in a moderately wooded area of the park and offer campers both shade and, surprisingly for a facility this large, a small degree of privacy between sites. Painterville Creek runs along the backside of the campground but a foot bridge crosses it and on the other side a trail climbs around Mt. Randal, a wooded dune, to the day-use beach area. Along with tables and fire rings, each loop has a restroom with showers. A sanitation station is located near the registration building.

Day-use Facilities: Separated from the rest of the park by several towering dunes is the day-use beach areas of the park. There is parking for 2,100 cars along Lake Michigan but the area still fills up on summer weekends and occasionally the staff sets up overflow parking for another 600 vehicles before they start turning people away. The popularity of the

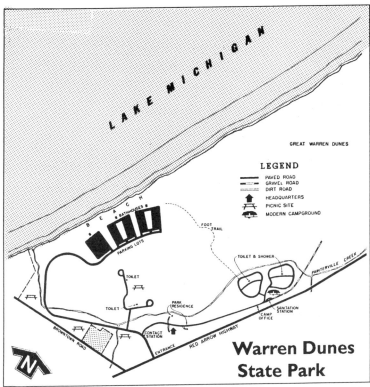

LAKE MICHIGAN

GREAT WARREN DUNES

LEGEND

PAVED ROAD
GRAVEL ROAD
DIRT ROAD
HEADQUARTERS
PICNIC SITE
MODERN CAMPGROUND

B E A C H

BATHHOUSES

FOOT TRAIL

PARKING LOTS

TOILET

TOILET & SHOWER

PAINTERVILLE CREEK

PARK RESIDENCE

SANITATION STATION

TOILET

CAMP OFFICE

BROWNTOWN ROAD

CONTACT STATION

ENTRANCE   RED ARROW HIGHWAY

**Warren Dunes
State Park**

beach is easy to understand. The wide sandy beach is bordered by towering dunes on one side and the light blue waters of Lake Michigan on the other. In between are three bathhouses. The park also has a wooded picnic area where a dune is li spilling among the tables.

Hiking: The park has a 4.5-mile network of maintained trails that forms a large loop from the modern campground through its natural area and then back along the shoreline to the day-use beach area. From here you climb around Mt. Randal to return to the campground. Cross the footbridge over Painterville Creek to pick up the trail.

Season: The campground is open year-round but filled weekends from May through October and daily during the summer. The park uses a priority number system for campers waiting for an open site on a first-come-first-serve basis and occasionally has even set-up an "overflow campground" when private facilities in the area are filled. Best bet, however, is to make reservations far in advance of your trip.

GRAND HAVEN
STATE PARK

Region: Lake Michigan
Nearest Community: Grand Haven
Sites: 182 **Reservations:** Yes
Fee: $13 plus a vehicle entry fee
Information: Park headquarters (616) 842-6020

Sites at Grand Haven State Park are little more then a cement slab with no trees, no vegetation to keep the blowing sand at bay and little privacy from your neighbor who is but four feet away. There are no maintained trails at this park, no boat launch and it's located in one of the most popular tourist towns along Lake Michigan.

But what a beach! Many consider Grand Haven's 2,500-foot strip of Lake Michigan the finest beach in the state and is one reason why this park draws more than 1.3 million visitors annually. The other is Grand Haven, the town. The park is connected to the restaurants and shops of downtown Grand Haven by Lighthouse Connector Park, a delightful boardwalk along the Grand River that ends with a popular fishing pier and picturesque Grand Haven Lighthouse in Lake Michigan.

If an urban campground is what you like, Grand Haven is a gem.

Directions: The park is a mile southwest of US-31 in Grand Haven along Harbor Drive. From US-31 follow directional signs to "Downtown."

Campground: Grand Haven has 182 modern sites in a setting that is open with no shade and little space between campers. A few sites actually border the beach with an open view of Lake Michigan and all of them are a short walk away from the surf. Each site has a table and hookup but no fire rings or grills of any kind. Showers, modern restrooms and a sanitation station round out the facilities.

Day-use Facilities: Grand Haven's beach posses some of the finest sand along Lake Michigan and during the summer is a colorful scene with wind surfers, swimmers, sunbathers and kite flyers. There is day parking for 800 vehicles but often on weekends in July and August the lot fills and additional cars are turned away. Park downtown and for a small fee you can hop aboard the city trolley bus. Also located within the day-use area

Grand Haven Lighthouse and its pier, a popular fishing spot during the summer with campers staying at the state park.

are picnic facilities, play equipment, bathhouse and a concession store.

Fishing: Adjacent to the park is historical Grand Haven Lighthouse and a pier connecting it to the boardwalk along Grand River. This is one of many popular Great Lakes fishing piers with anglers jigging for perch during the summer and casting spoons and plugs for brown trout, steelhead and salmon during the fall and spring.

The park maintains a fishermen's parking lot with a posted entrance off Harbor Drive and opens it at 5 a.m. as for early morning anglers. Lake Michigan is a noted deepwater fishery for salmon and steelhead although in recent years the catch has been down. There is no ramp facility in the park but there are public boat ramps and marinas in the city. A number of charter boat captains work out of Chinook Pier.

Season: Grand Haven's campground is open from April through October. Due to the park's overwhelming popularity, the staff holds a reservation lottery on the first working day in January for the following summer. Only written requests are entered in the lottery and they must be postmarked after Dec. 20 and received by Dec. 31. The park fills 72 percent of its sites by advance reservations and the rest are handed out on a first-come-first-serve basis. But be prepared to take a number and wait two or three days for an open site if you arrive without a reservation. To reserve a site send the dates you wish to Grand Haven State Park, 1001 Harbor Drive, Grand Haven, MI 49417.

6 P.J. HOFFMASTER
STATE PARK

Region: Lake Michigan
Nearest Community: Muskegon
Sites: 333   **Reservations:** Yes
Fee: $13 plus a vehicle entry fee
Information: Park headquarters (616) 798-3711

Like many Lake Michigan state parks, P.J. Hoffmaster features a wide and sandy beach and a rolling terrain of both wooded and open dunes. But unlike most units along Michigan's Gold Coast, P.J. Hoffmaster is large enough to be more than a campground and a beach.

The 1,043-acre park includes 2.5-miles of undeveloped shoreline, a 10-mile network of trails, even a "quiet area" where often it's possible to escape the summer crush of tourists found elsewhere along this side of the state. P.J. Hoffmaster also has a huge campground of several hundred modern sites that, despite the large number, still maintains something of a rustic wooded appearance.

What P.J. Hoffmaster does share with the other Lake Michigan state parks is the difficulty of booking a site. Don't expect to show up on a Thursday in mid-July and obtain a site. Advance reservations are strongly recommended during the summer season but they are far easier to book here than at Grand Haven State Park just down the shore. And P.J. Hoffmaster is definitely worth a little pre-vacation planning.

Directions: The park is located just south of Muskegon. From I-96 depart at exit 4 and head south on 148th Avenue and then immediately turn west (right) onto Pontaluna Road, which ends in 6 miles at the park entrance.

Campground: Located at the north end of the park in a wooded valley, the campground has 333 sites on four loops. The loops are well forested in hardwoods and pines and being dune country the sites are in a sandy area covered with needles but little undergrowth.

The largest loop (sites 188-333), the only one on the south side of Little Black Creek, is especially nice as many of the sites back up to a steep wooded dune while others overlook the clear, gently flowing stream. The trees here are older pines and hardwoods for a more natural setting than

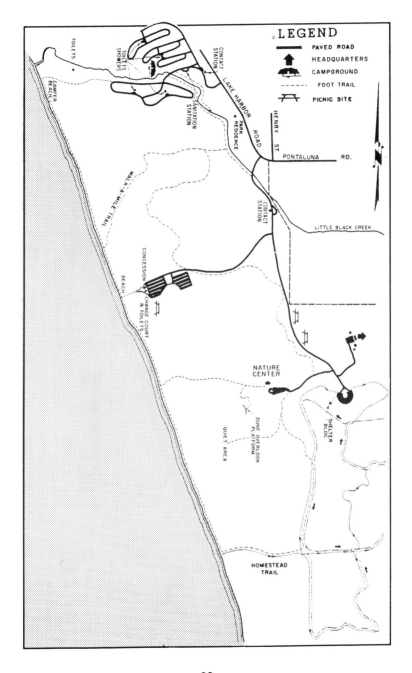

LEGEND
PAVED ROAD
HEADQUARTERS
CAMPGROUND
FOOT TRAIL
PICNIC SITE

the red pine plantation that two other loops are located in. A 0.25-mile trail leads from the back of this loop to a camper's beach on Lake Michigan.

Sites have tables, fire rings and electric hook-ups while four shower\restrooms service the campground. A sanitation station for trailers is located just beyond the contact station.

Day-use Facilities: P.J. Hoffmaster maintains a day-use area on Lake Michigan with parking for 550 cars. The facility includes a bathhouse, concession store and picnic areas near a golden stretch of Lake

Trilliums

Michigan beach. Further south along the park road are additional picnic areas in a wooded setting and Gillette Nature Center. Built in 1976 as Michigan's sand dune interpretive center, the two-story building is in fact overshadowed by a huge, wind-blown dune. The center features an exhibit hall, 82-seat theater and a hands-on display area, all related to dunes and the biological zones that surround them. Gillette (Tel. 616-798-3573) is open year-round, Tuesday through Sunday. In the summer, the hours are 9 a.m. to 6 p.m.

Hiking: The park is large enough to be laced by a 10-mile network of foot trails that loop through the wooded dunes and along the Lake Michigan shoreline. The most popular walk is *Dune Climb Stairway* that departs from Gillette Nature Center and follows a long stairway to the top of a high sand dune for a panorama of the park. The best hike in the park is *Homestead Trail*, a 3.5-mile loop that also departs from the nature center and winds through a designated natural area, passes a spur to the park's Quiet Area and ends up on Lake Michigan.

Reservations: Like most other Lake Michigan state parks, P.J. Hoffmaster fills up daily from mid-June through most of August. Reservations are accepted beginning the first working day in January for the following summer and 50 percent of the sites are reserved in advance. A priority number system is used for people waiting for a site during the summer on a first-come-first-serve basis.

7 LAKE MICHIGAN
MUSKEGON STATE PARK

Region: Lake Michigan
Nearest Community: North Muskegon
Sites: 170   **Reservations:** Yes
Fee: $10 plus vehicle entry fee
Information: Park headquarters (616) 744-3480

One of the oldest campgrounds on the west side of the state is at Muskegon State Park. The park's Lake Michigan Campground was constructed in the 1930s, before the advent of motorhomes and pop-up trailers. Subsequently this modern facility is atypical, lacking that plowed-out, paved-over look of many state park campgrounds. If you can maneuver your trailer into the site, this is a delightful place to camp.

The 1,357-acre park is a peninsula surrounded by Lake Michigan on one side and Muskegon Lake on the other and is best known as the home of the only luge run in the Lower Peninsula. But of more interest to summer campers is the trail network that winds through wooded dunes and the almost 3 miles of wide sandy beach.

Directions: The park is five miles west of North Muskegon. From US-31 depart at M-120 and head southwest, following park signs to Memorial Drive, which terminates at the park's south entrance. Lake Michigan Campground is closer to the north entrance reached by following Scenic Drive south from Whitehall.

Campground: The Lake Michigan campground has 170 sites on a loop of several lanes. The pre-motorhome era facility is neither level nor is it easy to pull trailers into many of the sites and large RVs are sent down to Muskegon Lake campground at the south end of the park. The gently rolling area at Lake Michigan campground is well wooded in deciduous trees and bordered to the west by wind-blown sand dunes. There are no sites directly on the water but the beautiful Great Lake shoreline is only a short walk away. The facility has tables, fire rings, two restrooms with showers and a sanitation station.

Day-use Facilities: The park has two day-use areas. The most popular one is on Lake Michigan where there is parking for 600 vehicles,

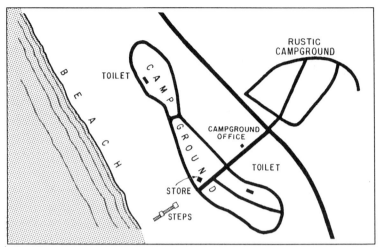

a bathhouse-store and a wide sandy beach that is typical for this side of the state. The second is on Snug Harbor on Muskegon Lake near the south entrance of the park. Snug Harbor has tables, pedestal grills, a shelter and a small sandy beach though the water here is not nearly as desirable as Lake Michigan.

Fishing: There are two improved boat launches with docks and cement ramps within the park. Both are on Muskegon Lake, one in the Snug Harbor day-use area and the other in the nearby modern campground. Boaters then use Ship Canal to gain quick access into Lake Michigan. Fishing opportunities abound in this park. The 4,150-acre Muskegon Lake is noted for its perch and bass as well as being stocked annually with walleye. Shore anglers can use piers in Snug Harbor or along Ship Canal or follow the beach south to reach a rocky breakwall where the catch is perch during the summer and steelhead and salmon in the spring and late fall.

Hiking: The park maintains a network of 4.5-miles of trails through a terrain of forested lowlands and hills. Most of the network is a large loop with parking and a trailhead in the rustic campground across Scenic Drive from Lake Michigan Campground.

Reservations: Lake Michigan Campground is not as popular as the one on Muskegon Lake, thus it's lower nightly fee. Still it fills up weekends from July through Labor Day, usually by Thursday afternoon. Telephone reservations can be obtained Monday through Friday at the park office and should be made at least seven days prior to the desired dates.

8 CHARLES MEARS
STATE PARK

Region: Lake Michigan
Nearest Community: Pentwater
Sites: 180   **Reservations:** Yes
Fee: $13 plus a vehicle entry fee
Information: Park headquarters (616) 869-2051

It might be small at only 50 acres in size, but Charles Mears State Park is still one of the most popular campgrounds in the entire state. As an urban campground, it's hard to match. It's tucked away on a beach of its own, away from the traffic of Business US-31, but within a short walk are the shops, stores and restaurants of downtown Pentwater, a popular tourist town.

Mears is a "destination campground" as opposed to a stopover on the way up north. People work so hard or wait so long to get a site they end up staying here four to five days on the average. Plan ahead if you want to make this park a part of your summer vacation.

Directions: From US-31, follow Business US-31 through Pentwater and look for state park signs. Mears is four blocks from the downtown area.

Campground: Mears has 180 sites that feature not only electric hookups but also paved pads for recreational vehicles because the campground is little more than an open sandy area with little to no shade. Nor do any of the sites overlook Lake Michigan like at Grand Haven as a string of dunes separate them from the beach. Within the campground are two modern restrooms with showers, a sanitation station and a fish cleaning hut.

Day-use Facilities: Mears has a beautiful beach while the small dunes that border it are a great place to catch the a Great Lakes sunset. The day-use area has a shelter, bathhouse, beach volleyball courts and play equipment, concession store and picnic area. Often on summer weekends the parking lot will fill and all other visitors must park elsewhere in town and walk in.

Fishing: Adjacent to the park is Pentwater Pier, where anglers cast for perch and smallmouth bass during the summer. There is no boat ramp in the park but public facilities are located downtown and Pentwater is a popular port for deepwater fishing for salmon and steelhead in Lake Michigan. If you don't have a boat, several charter captains work out of Pentwater.

Hiking: There is a half mile of trail that winds around to the top of Old Baldy, a wooded and partially wind-blown sand dune that provides an excellent view of the Lake Michigan shoreline, the town of Pentwater and its extensive boat harbor.

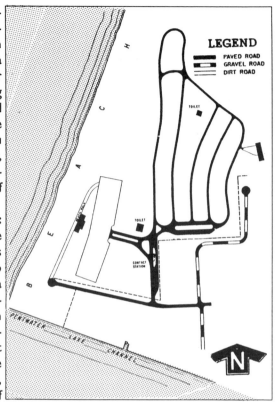

LEGEND
PAVED ROAD
GRAVEL ROAD
DIRT ROAD

Season: Mears is open April through October and is virtually filled every day from late June to mid-August. Mail-in reservations are accepted after Dec. 20 for the following year and, because of the overwhelming demand for summer dates, are drawn on a lottery basis on the first working day of January. Most of the pre-reserved sites are claimed at that time or soon afterwards by phone reservations.

Reservations claim 75 percent of the sites. The rest are handed out on a first-come-first-serve basis during the summer and visitors are encouraged to show up when the contact station opens at 8 a.m. to receive a priority number. It often takes three to four days to get a site after receiving your number. Send written reservation requests to Mears State Park, P.O. Box 370, Pentwater, MI 49449.

LUDINGTON
STATE PARK

Region: Lake Michigan
Nearest Community: Ludington
Sites: 399   **Reservations:** Yes
Fee: $13 plus vehicle entry fee
Information: Park headquarters (616) 843-8671

Like many state parks along Lake Michigan, Ludington State Park is a popular unit and a tough place to get a site without a reservation or waiting a day or two. Unlike most other parks, however, once you have set up camp, it's easy to escape the crowds in this wonderful stretch of shoreline, dunes and forest.

At 5,200 acres, Ludington is the largest state park on Lake Michigan and second largest in the Lower Peninsula. It includes 5.5 miles of Great Lake shoreline, another 4 miles along popular Hamlin Lake and a 1,699-acre Wilderness Natural Area that is undeveloped and forms a border with Nordhouse Dunes Wilderness to the north.

The popularity of this park is easy to understand. There are paved bike paths, the Great Lakes Interpretive Center to visit, an 18-mile network of hiking trails and Big Point Sable Lighthouse, a photographer's delight with it's distinctive black and white tower. All this accounts for the more than 700,000 people that visit the park annually with the vast majority arriving from May through September. But if the crowds turn you off then just start hiking the Lake Michigan shoreline north and eventually the beach towels, the bikes the bustle and even the foot prints in the sand disappear.

Directions: The state park is 8.5 miles north Ludington at the end of M-116.

Campground: The park has three separate campgrounds that stretch from Lake Michigan to Hamlin Lake on the north side of the Big Sable River. All three are well wooded, offering shady sites, and are connected to each other and the day-use areas by the paved bike paths. There is little privacy between sites but there is just enough space and trees to avoid a campground that looks like a used RV lot.

Pines Campground has 118 sites and is closest to Lake Michigan, separated by the golden beach by only a sand dune, thus the popularity for the west side of the loop. *Cedar Campground* is a pair of loops of 120 sites and located in the middle and Beachwood Campground has 171 sites located just north of the Hamlin Lake day-use area.

Beachwood is my personal choice when setting up camp. It's a figure-eight loop where the sites surround forested knolls and low dunes in the middle. On the east side the sites border a low dune that can be climbed for a pleasant view of Hamlin Lake and its many islands and lagoons as well as provide direct access to the Beachwood Trail. A handful of sites at the northeast corner of the loop actually lookout onto Lost Lake, the only place in the park where a waterfront view is possible. Sites include tables and fire rings while four restroom/shower buildings, including two in Beechwood, service the campgrounds. A sanitation station is located near the bathhouse.

Day-Use Facilities: There are two beaches in the park, one on Lake Michigan, just north of where the Big Sable River empties into the Great Lake and the second on Hamlin Lake. Both have parking and a bathhouse but early in the summer the Hamlin beach is more popular because its water warms up quicker. M-116 follows Lake Michigan for almost 3 miles after entering the park and it's common for visitors to just pull over along the road to enjoy a stretch of beach.

The park's nature center on the south side of Big Sable River was recently renovated as the Great Lakes Interpretive Center with displays, exhibits and a slide presentation focusing on Michigan's most famous lakes. The center is open daily from Memorial Day through Labor Day from 10 a.m. to 5:30 p.m.

Fishing: Hamlin Lake, with its many coves, inlets and bayous, is a renowned warmwater fishery. There is heavy spawning of northern pike and tiger muskellunge in the shallow coves, and anglers frequently have landed muskies over 15 pounds. The 4,490-acre lake, which is nearly 10 miles long, is also noted for bass and bluegill as well. The lake has been stocked with tiger muskies since the early 1980s and in 1987 a walleye stocking program began. The park maintains an improved boat ramp on the inland lake near the day-use area with parking for 75 trailers and vehicles and a fish cleaning station near the Lake Michigan beachhouse. Other fishing activity in the park includes surf fishing in the early spring and October for salmon and trout off the Lake Michigan shoreline.

Hiking: The park boasts a well-posted trail network, featuring a number of stone shelters that make an ideal place to enjoy lunch. There

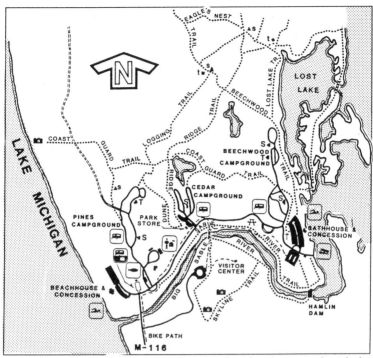

are 11 named and color-coded trails within the 18-mile network with the shortest and most spectacular located south of the Big Sable River. The *Skyline Interpretive Trail* is less than half-mile long but involves a steep winding stairway to the top of a dune where a boardwalk has been constructed along the crest. How steep is the dune? Helicopters were needed to carry the lumber to the top. But the view from the boardwalk is spectacular and along the way there are numbered interpretive posts that correspond to a brochure available at each of the three stairways.

The rest of the trail system is north of the river with posted trailheads located in the campgrounds or the Hamlin Lake Day-use Area. Several trails can be combined for day-long loops through the unique terrain of the park's Wilderness Natural Area. The *Ridge and Island Trails* makes a 5.2-mile loop that features viewing the perched dunes above Hamlin Lake, winding around the inlets and bays along the lake and reaching a stone shelter at the halfway point. Plan on three to four hours for the trek.

Equally scenic is to follow the *Logging and Lighthouse trails* out to Big Point Sable Lighthouse and then return along the beach. It would be a

The start of the Skyline Trail at Ludington State Park.

round trip of 4.8 miles that includes viewing the historic lighthouse and some wonderful beachcombing for driftwood along the point.

Season: The campgrounds are open all year and full daily from early June through Labor Day weekend. Most reservation requests made in January and February for the following summer can be accommodated, but a lottery is held on the first working day of January for the Fourth of July weekend, by far the most heavily requested period of the year. Reservations require that you book at least two nights and can be obtained during the winter by sending a request to Ludington State Park, P.O. Box 709, Lundington, MI 49431 or by calling the park.

The park staff reserves only 50 percent of the sites and during the summer maintains a priority number list for those waiting for a site on a first-come-first-serve basis. Campers should expect to wait, and stay elsewhere, for two days before they can obtain a site.

10 PORT CRESCENT STATE PARK

Region: Lake Huron
Nearest Community: Port Austin
Sites: 181   **Reservations:** Yes
Fee: $13 plus a vehicle entry fee
Information: Park headquarters (517) 738-8663

In the mid-1800s Port Crescent was a booming lumbering town of almost 700 residents, known for its salt wells, fine sand and good docks. Today it's one of the most scenic state parks along Lake Huron known for having the only "true dunes" on the east side of the state. The wind-blown, open dunes are located west of the park's day-use area and drop down to the shoreline. They are nowhere near the size of those along Lake Michigan but they are still an interesting area to wander through. And to small children sand dunes are sand dunes regardless of their size.

The 565-acre unit also includes 3 miles of almost pure white beach along Saginaw Bay, a wooded interior of jack pine and oak, a scenic network of hiking trails and a campground overlooking the bay that

The sand dunes in Port Crescent State Park along Saginaw Bay.

includes 25 beachfront sites.

Directions: The park is 5 miles southwest of Port Austin along M-25.

Campground: Port Crescent's campground is located in the eastern half of the park in a hilly section forested in oak and bordered on one side by the Old Pinnebog River Channel and the other by M-25. Many sites have a partial view of Saginaw Bay and 25 of them are right off the beach. These, understandably, are not only the most popular sites in the park but some of the most scenic on the east side of the state. They are in such high demand during the summer that the park has devised a lot-move procedure to allow campers to sign-up for them after they have already arrived at the campground. Facilities include tables, fire rings, two restrooms with showers and a sanitation station.

Day-use Facilities: The west half of the park is a day-use area and is separated from the campground and hiking trails by the Pinnebog River. The area includes two picnic grounds along the river, a shelter that can be rented near the beach, a fitness trail nearby and limited play equipment. A boardwalk leads from the shelter to the beach, one of the finest along Lake Huron, passing along the way small decks with picnic tables perched on top of the low dunes.

Fishing: While Saginaw Bay is renowned for its walleye and perch fishery, the Pinnebog River is fished by shore anglers for bass, panfish and northern pike during the summer and occasionally for Chinook salmon in September and October by tossing spoons and spawn. In the day-use area there is a launch for hand-carried boats and some barrier-free fishing piers over the river. Perch anglers should head to Port Austin and catch the morning or afternoon run of the perch party boat, *Miss Port Austin,* (517-738-5271).

Hiking: Port Crescent has three miles of foot trails in an isolated area between the Pinnebog River and the Old Pinnebog River Channel. You can reach one trailhead by a beach access next to site 119 and then tiptoe through the channel where it empties into the bay. On the other side is a yellow trail marker. The entire loop is a 2.3-mile walk that passes several scenic viewing points of the shoreline and the Pinnebog River. By using the cut-off spur you can shorten it to a 1.3-mile walk.

Season: Port Crescent is open from April 15 to Oct. 15. The campground is filled most weekends during the summer and often daily from mid-July to early August. Best time to check in without a reservation is Sunday and Monday.

11

PINCONNING
COUNTY PARK

Region: Lake Huron
Nearest Community: Pinconning
Sites: 43   **Reservations:** Yes
Fee: $7.50 plus vehicle entry fee
Information: Bay County Reacreation (517) 893-5531

One of the newest, most pleasant and, best of all, least crowded modern campground in the state is Pinconning County Park along the Saginaw Bay. The park is only 3 miles from I-75 but most likely too far south for many campers to consider stopping for the night.

Too bad. This is a scenic park with a beach, improved boat launch, some short but interesting hiking trails and many sites that overlook a small bay and peninsula bordering Saginaw Bay.

Directions: From I-75 turn off at Pinconning (exit 181), 21 miles north of Bay City. Head east on Pinconning Road, through the town of Pinconning, and in 3 miles the road ends at the park entrance.

Campground: Pinconning is a single loop of 43 sites in an open grassy area that is shaded by giant oak trees. Half the sites are along the Bay and some of them have a clear view of the water while the others are tucked behind a wall of cattails. The rest border the forest that surrounds the campground. Facilities include fire rings, tables, a restroom with showers and a sanitation station. Also located in the campground is an observation tower that is ideal for viewing the waterfowl and other birds that thrive in the back bay.

The nightly fee is $7.50 for a full hook-up and $5.50 for those who don't need electricity. There is also a $1 vehicle entry fee.

Day-Use Facilities: Pinconning has a sandy beach but in recent years the water level had dropped in the Bay making it muddy and unattractive to swimmers. Bay County plans to rectify the situation, however, by extending the beach. Also within the picnic area is a shelter, tables, pedestal grills, play equipment and an open view of Saginaw Bay.

Fishing: There is also a cement boat launch and dock in the day-use area. Again the low water level has hampered boaters but officials plan to dredge a channel for them into deeper water from the launch. Saginaw

Bay is renowned for its walleye and perch fisheries while in the small bay off the campground anglers target mostly large and smallmouth bass.

Hiking: The park has four posted trails, all short excursions into the surrounding woods and marshes. The most interesting by far is the *Marsh Trail*, a round trip of 0.6 mile through the extensive cattail marshes that enclose the bay. The path passes views of the water and a small observation deck before turning around at a wooden bridge.

Season: The operating season for the campground varies on demand and weather but is usually open from May through October. Reservations can be booked in advance by calling the park office at (517) 879-5050 but this is a lightly used facility that rarely fills up, even on the weekends.

12 TAWAS POINT
STATE PARK

Region: Lake Huron
Nearest Community: East Tawas
Sites: 210   **Reservations:** Yes
Fee: $10 plus a vehicle entry fee
Information: Park headquarters (517) 362-5041

Tawas Point is a popular state park that combines a beautiful beach within walking distance of a large campground and both are crowned by a classic lighthouse. The 185-acre park is the end of a sandy spit that separates Tawas Bay from Lake Huron and prompts a few people to call it "the Cape Code of the Midwest."

That's stretching it a bit, but Tawas Point is definitely a scenic area and even has a short trail to the end of the spit and back. The area also attracts birders from around the state as it is an important landfall for birds migrating across Saginaw Bay. The contact station can provide a birding check list.

Directions: The park is 3.5 miles north of East Tawas. Follow US-23 just northeast of the town and then turn east onto Tawas Point Road and follow signs to the park entrance.

Campground: Tawas Point is an open campground with little shade or privacy between parties. A handful of sites overlook a small beach along

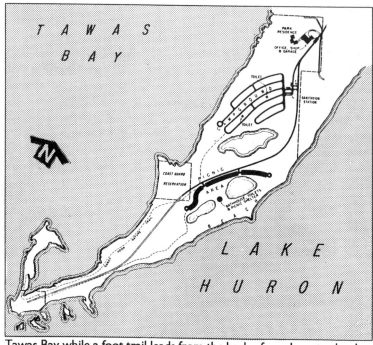

Tawas Bay while a foot trail leads from the back of one loop to the day-use area beach along Lake Huron. Facilities include two restrooms with showers, play equipment and a sanitation station within the campground and fire rings and tables at each site.

Day-use Facilities: The park's day-use beach is along Lake Huron where the sand is almost pure white and stretches more than 300 feet from where you park your car to where the waves are gently washing ashore. Located here is a bathhouse, picnic shelter and more play equipment. The area is surrounded by several small ponds that occasionally attracts the interest of young anglers.

Hiking: Beginning at the day-use parking lot, near the lighthouse, is the *Sandy Hook Nature Trail*, a 1.5-mile loop to the end of the point. Its most scenic portion by far is along Lake Huron where you pass several small islets and skirt the tops of some small, very small, dunes.

Season: The campground is open from mid-April to mid-October and through most of the summer it's filled from Thursday until Sunday. In July, expect it to be filled any day of the week. Reservations are important if you want to plan a vacation around this campground.

HARRISVILLE
STATE PARK

Region: Lake Huron
Nearest Community: Harrisville
Sites: 299 **Reservations:** Yes
Fee: $10 plus vehicle entry fee
Information: Park headquarters (517) 724-5126

Harrisville State Park is proof that, despite being on Michigan's Gold Coast, Lake Michigan campgrounds do not have a monopoly on wide sandy beaches. The outstanding feature of this 97-acre park is its half mile-long stretch of Lake Huron shoreline where its sugar-like sand is more than 30 yards wide in most places. Here you take a refreshing dip in the cooling waters of the Great Lake, lay out in the sun or, if you're lucky, set up camp at a beachfront campsite.

Although the park has a day-use area and even a nature trail, its relatively small size limits the facilities that other larger units offer. But there is a bike path that connects it with Harrisville, a quaint town during the summer with small restaurants, ice cream parlors, gift shops and the Harrisville Harbor where you can watch charter fishing boats return with their daily catch of salmon and trout.

Directions: The state park is half mile south of the town of Harrisville with an entrance right off US-23.

Campground: The park has a single campground of several paved loops in a lightly forested area of pine and cedar. Sites feature hook-ups, tables and fire pits and are within view of each other but not crammed together. By far the most popular sites are number 52 through 102, located right along the lake where your tent or trailer would be in the shade of the trees but your beach blanket only a few yards away. These are some of the best places to camp along Lake Huron and obtaining a site usually requires changing sites once you have arrived.

Along with a pair of bathroom and shower buildings, the campground features a Rent-A-Tent that families can obtain, a rustic cabin (see page 177) and the two trailheads to the Cedar Run Nature Trail.

Day-use Facilities: At the south end of the park is a day-use area with a bathhouse, shelter, picnic tables, playground equipment, and, of course, more of that wide, beautiful beach and Lake Huron surf. Here you

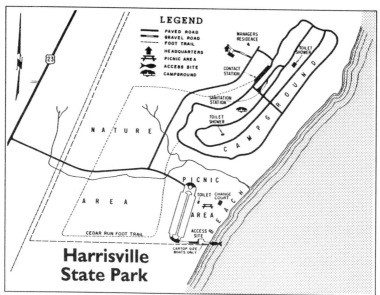

LEGEND
PAVED ROAD
GRAVEL ROAD
FOOT TRAIL
HEADQUARTERS
PICNIC AREA
ACCESS SITE
CAMPGROUND

MANAGERS RESIDENCE

TOILET SHOWER

CONTACT STATION

SANITATION STATION

TOILET SHOWER

N A T U R E

C A M P G R O U N D

P I C N I C

TOILET   CHANGE COURT

A R E A

A R E A

B E A C H

CEDAR RUN FOOT TRAIL

ACCESS SITE

CARTOP SIZE BOATS ONLY

Harrisville State Park

can set up a lounge chair, take in the sun or watch iron ore freighters pass by on the horizon. The bike/foot path begins near the entrance of the campground and is a paved trail that extends a half mile north to Harrisville, ending near First Street.

Fishing: Lake Huron is a noted deepwater fishery for salmon and lake trout and charters can be arranged at the Harrisville Harbor or bait shops in town. There is an unimproved launch for cartop and other hand-carried boats next to the park's day-use area but you need to go to town for anything bigger. Actually the only fishing activity within the park are surf anglers who work the beaches during the fall for salmon and brown trout feeding in the shallows.

Hiking: Departing and returning from the campground is the *Cedar Run Nature Trail*, a mile-long loop that takes 30 to 45 minutes to enjoy. There are 14 numbered posts on the trail and an interpretive brochure, obtained from the contact station, points out different species of trees.

Season: Harrisville is open from mid-April to the end of October. The campground is often filled on the weekends by Friday afternoon and sometimes by Thursday afternoon. The staff begins accepting written reservations on Jan. 1 for the following summer and reserves 75 percent of its campground in advance. Send requests to Harrisville State Park, P.O. Box 326, Harrisville, MI 48740.

14 HAYES STATE PARK

Region: Heartland
Nearest Community: Clinton
Sites: 210   **Reservations:** Yes
Fee: $10 plus vehicle entry permit
Information: Park headquarters (517) 467-7401

Travel along US-12 through the heart of the Irish Hills and you'll pass adventure golf, go-cart tracks, a theme park dedicated to dinosaurs and another one called Stagecoach USA. But there is a haven from all of these tourist traps and that's W.J. Hayes State Park. The 654-acre park is located on the banks of both Wampler's and Round Lake and has preserved a slice of the hills that reminded Irish settlers of their homeland in the 19th century.

W.J. Hayes has an excellent campground, beach area, boat launches on both lakes, even a wooded hiking trail. It's a haven from the plastic tyrannosaurus and other summer trappings of the Irish Hills except the tourists themselves. This is an extremely popular state park unit where even the beach area gets filled in August.

Directions: W.J. Hayes is located 9 miles west of Clinton at the junction of US-12 and M-124. The state highway actually splits the park in half.

Campground: The 210-site facility is composed of many loops on both the south and west shore of Round Lake, totally separated from the beach and day-use area on Wampler's. The first loop, sites 1-53, is on the west side with many sites within site of M-124. The end of the loop, however, is on a bluff above the lake and site 24 and 25 actually have a clear view of the water.

The rest of the campground is on the south side of the lake and sites 54-158 are located in a semi-open but hilly area. The sites are close to each other but shaded by towering oaks and the rolling terrain makes this large campground much more private than it would be otherwise. Sites 118-136 are off by themselves on a hillside loop overlooking a marsh area. The final loop are primitive sites 159-210 and the first few are the most popular ones in the park, located along the lake's wooded shoreline and

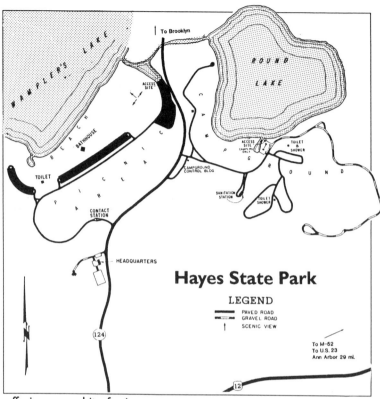

Hayes State Park

LEGEND

— PAVED ROAD
GRAVEL ROAD
↑ SCENIC VIEW

To M-52
To U.S. 23
Ann Arbor 29 mi.

offering a rare bit of privacy.

Day-use Facilities: The day-use area, the site of a Civilian Conservation Corps camp in the mid-1930s, is across M-124 from the campground and features a long, though rather thin beach bordered by a wide grassy area. There is also play equipment, picnic facilities, horseshoe pits, baseball field, bathhouse and a concession stand that runs a boat rental during the summer. The area is served by a 900-vehicle parking area and it still fills up about every Sunday afternoon in July. Additional vehicles are turned away.

Fishing: There are improved boat launches with cement ramps, docks and parking areas in both the day-use area and the campground. The one on Round Lake is for campers only, but a channel between the two lakes allows easy access from one to the other. Wampler's at 780 acres is considerably larger than Round and is known as one of southern Michigan's best smallmouth bass lakes as well as supporting good fisheries for perch and bluegill. But fishing pressure is intense during the summer and the lake is popular with recreational boaters as well. Round Lake, with it's no-wake regulation is quieter and supports the same species. But the 90-acre lake is usually not as productive as Wamplers.

Hiking: Hayes has a 2-mile path that departs from the west end of the campground into the southern half of the park, a wooded area of rolling hills.

Season: W.J. Hayes draws more than 600,000 visitors annually and from Memorial Day to Labor Day the campground is filled by Friday afternoon or sooner if there is an event at nearby Michigan International Speedway. Reservations can be made in advance by calling the park headquarters and you can usually get a site Sunday through Wednesday. Mid to late October is an ideal time to camp here and the facility is open from April through October.

15
COLDBROOK
KALAMAZOO COUNTY PARKS

Region: Heartland
Nearest Community: Climax
Sites: 29   **Reservations:** Yes
Fee: $10 plus a vehicle entry permit
Information: Kalamazoo County Parks (616) 383-8778

At the headwaters of the Portage River is Portage and Blue lakes, a sprawling body of water of many peninsulas, bays, channels and the site of a modern campground that lies just a few miles off I-94 between Battle Creek and Kalamazoo. Coldbrook County Park is a 275-acre facility operated by Kalamazoo County with both rustic and modern sites.

The park is spread along the south and east shore of Portage Lake and totally encloses Blue Lake. Much of the west half of lakes are a shallow marshy area, filled with lily pads and other aquatic plants that attracts a variety of waterfowl during the spring and fall migrations.

Directions: Coldbrook is just south of I-94, 8 miles east of Kalamazoo along MN Avenue. From the east, depart at exit 92, Business I-94 for Battle Creek, but head south for the town of Climax. In 2 miles you'll merge onto MN Avenue and the entrance of the park is a mile west along the road.

Campground: Coldbrook has both modern sites and a rustic loop, each on a small peninsula of their own on the southwest corner of Portage Lake. The 29 modern sites are close together in an open grassy area with only a few small trees and little shade. There is a single restroom with showers along with grills, tables, a sanitation station and limited play equipment. A bridge crosses the narrow channel into Blue Lake to the picnic area on the other side.

The rustic portion of the campground has 21 sites in a wooded area of small hardwoods with the sites well shaded but still close together. This loop has vault toilets, fire grills, table and a hand pump for water while a foot trail connects it with the rest of the park.

Day-use Facilities: A pleasant picnic area with a large shelter, play equipment and tables and grills is located on a wooded hill overlooking both Blue and Portage Lake. Further up the park road is another shelter, ball field and finally the beach area with its bathhouse, parking for additional vehicles and more tables and grills. On the east side of Portage Lake, where the beach is located, the water is deep and clear. The beach contains very little sandy but is bordered by a pleasant grassy area.

Fishing: An improved boat launch with cement ramp and dock is situated next to the beach and includes its own parking area. There is a no wake regulation between the narrow channels of the lakes and no high speed boating or water skiing is allowed from 7:30 p.m. to 11 a.m. The shoreline of these lakes are completely undeveloped and anglers will work the east side of Portage for a variety of fish, including bass and panfish.

Hiking: A posted trail system departs from the beach area and skirts the park shoreline, passing through the picnic area and both campgrounds before crossing a dike at the rustic loop to a woods on the west side.

Season: Coldbrook is open from Memorial Day through October, charges $8 for a rustic site and a $1 less for county residents. Call the Kalamazoo County parks office to reserve sites but they must be booked two weeks in advance. The campground is often filled on summer weekends.

16

PARIS
MECOSTA COUNTY PARKS

Region: Heartland
Nearest Community: Paris
Sites: 68   **Reservations:** No
Fee: $8.75 plus vehicle entry permit
Information: Park office (616) 796-3420

In 1881, Michigan opened its second fish rearing facility near the town of Paris because of its excellent railroad connections with the rest of the state and abundant water source of the nearby Muskegon River. Biologists raised salmon and brown trout fingerlings which were then placed in milk cans (painted red so as not to confuse them with real milk cans) and shipped all over Michigan on railroad baggage cars.

The Paris Fish Hatchery went on to become the state's major supplier of salmon and trout and was even renovated and expanded in the mid-1930s before the Department of Natural Resources shut it down in 1964 as an outdated facility. But the impressive white building, ponds and raceways are still there and today are what make the Mecosta County park so unique.

Where else can you camp at a fish hatchery, look at huge trout, feed trout, even catch an 18-inch rainbow trout for dinner? The 15-acre park, which opened in 1976, also features a large picnic area, a canoe launch area, one of the state's newest rails-to-trails passing through, even a replica of the Eiffel Tower.

This is Paris, after all, isn't it?

Directions: Paris Park is 6 miles north of Big Rapids on Old US-131 (also labeled Northland Drive). From US-131 depart at exit 142 and head east on 19 Mile Road and then north on Northland Drive.

Campground: The modern facility has electric and water hook-ups along with heated restrooms and showers. The 68-sites are located in a semi-open grassy with scattered hardwoods. It's well shaded but offers little privacy and none of the sites are near the Muskegon River or have a view of the water.

Day-use Facilities: Across from the campground is a large day-use

The old fish hatchery at Paris County Park near Big Rapids.

area with a shelter, tables, pedestal grills, swings and other playground equipment. Park here and stroll through the old hatchery ponds and raceways which have been converted into an interesting wildlife area where you see a variety of semi-domesticated ducks, Canada geese and swans or some very impressive rainbow trout, some up to 10-pounds in weight. Both bird feed (dry corn) and fish feed (pellets) are available from dispensers for $.10 a handful while sidewalks, bridges and stone fences wind through the area and past a small replica of the Eiffel Tower.

Fishing: The Muskegon River is a renowned fishery and this far up stream anglers target trout in spring and fall and smallmouth bass during the summer.

But even of more interest to visitors are the trout ponds within the park. The old fish hatchery building is now occupied by a local trout farmer who stocks the ponds and runs a "fish-for-fee" concession. He supplies poles, bait and a net and inspiring anglers are allowed to fish the first trout pond. It looks easy but it's not. Those trout know when you're just tossing a pellet in and when there is a hook embedded in it. The experience is lots of fun for children, no fishing licenses are needed and the trout are excellent to eat. Most fish run between 12-14 inches but there are a few 18 inches and larger swimming around. The concession is open 10 a.m. to 6 p.m., Thursday through Sunday, from June through

August and weekends in May and September. Cost is $.30 an inch.

Canoeing: The park includes a canoe launch on the Muskegon River and parking for a limited number of vehicles. The paddle from Paris to Highbanks Park in Big Rapids is a 13-mile, four-hour trip through a mostly wide and easy river. Canoes or inner tubes can be rented in Big Rapids at *Sawmill Canoe Livery* (Tel. 616-796-6408), which will also provide transportation and pick-up from the campground.

Hiking: The newest rail-to-trail project passes through the park on its way from Cadillac to Big Rapids. The rails have already been pulled and a gravel path put in for hikers and mountain bikers. Eventually the route will extend to Grand Rapids with paved paths and rest stops in the same format as the Kal-Haven Trail near Kalamazoo.

Season: The campground is open from May to October or sometimes later depending on the weather. On the weekends it is busy but rarely filled and there is no problem obtaining a site Sunday through Wednesday.

17 PLATTE RIVER
SLEEPING BEAR DUNES
NATIONAL LAKESHORE

Region: Northwest
Nearest Community: Honor
Sites: 179   **Reservations:** No
Fee: $8-$15
Information: Park Headquarters (616) 326-5134

The newest modern campground in Michigan is also one of the oldest campgrounds and certainly one of the most expensive facilities. Platte River Campground was originally Benzie State Park until the DNR deeded it over to the National Park Service in 1975 as part of Sleeping Bear Dunes National Lakeshore.

In 1990 and 1991, the NPS closed down the rustic facility, spent almost $4 million in renovation and then opened it in May, 1992 as Michigan's newest modern facility. And what a facility! It's the state-of-the-art campground, providing modern, rustic and walk-in sites in one of the most beloved areas of the Lower Peninsula. As of 1992, the NPS was

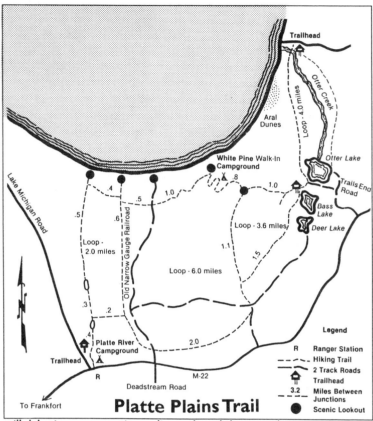

Platte Plains Trail

still debating a reservation policy and until then, you better arrive early to obtain site at Platte River. This one is destined to be a popular campground.

Directions: From the Sleeping Bear Dunes park headquarters (open daily 9 a.m. to 5 p.m.) on the corner of M-72 and M-22 in Empire, head south on M-22 and in 9.5 miles you'll reach the campground before crossing Platte River. From US-31, north of Beulah, head west on County Road 706 around the south side of Platte Lake and then north on M-22.

Campground: Platte River is a large facility of four paved loops in an area lightly forested predominantly in pines. Of the 179 sites, 96 of them have electric hook-ups and 53 others are rustic. None of the sites are near the water as Lake Michigan Road lies between the campground and the river. At the back of the campground there are 25 walk-in sites

Young hikers on the Platte Plains Trail network.

where you camp in a much more secluded area 50 yards from where you park your car. There are also group sites. Facilities include paved spurs, tables, fire rings, a sanitation station and modern restrooms with pay-to-use showers.

Day-use Facilities: The major change in the campground was re-routing Lake Michigan Road and rebuilding the picnic area on the shores of the Platte River. The picnic area now lies across the road from the campground and includes tables and grills within view of the water.

There is no swimming area within the campground but one of the most scenic beaches in the state lies less than two miles away at the west end of Lake Michigan Road. Here the Platte River empties into Lake Michigan, forming a delightful sandy split that is reached by wading through the shallow current. To the north is a view of undeveloped Platte Bay and Sleeping Bear Dune itself. One of the favorite activities at the beach is to float down the Platte River along the spit into Lake Michigan in an inner tube.

Fishing: Platte Bay is renown for its salmon and brown trout fishery during the spring and fall as the fish gather to spawn up the river. The deepwater fishery here is also very productive during the summer but the nearest Great Lakes boat launch is in Frankfort. The campground does have a fish cleaning station.

Hiking: *Platte Plains Trail* is a 15-mile network of trails with two

A family tackles the Dune Climb at Sleeping Bear Dunes National Lakeshore.

trailheads in the campground. The one at the back near the walk-in sites provides the quickest route to the beaches of Lake Michigan, a walk of little over a half mile. There is also a 6-mile loop that begins and ends at Platte River and within 2.4 miles passes the backcountry campsites of White Pine Campground.

Canoeing: The lower Platte River from the campground makes for an easy, 2-hour canoe trip while an equal number of people float it during the summer in an inner tube. It's averages only 3 feet in depth and along the way passes through a small lake before emptying into Lake Michigan. *Riverside Canoes* (Tel. 616-882-4072) can provide either canoes or inner tubes and are located across the river from the campground. During the height of summer you may want to reserve a boat in advance.

Season: Platte River is open year round but some facilities are seasonable. The fee rate is $15 for modern sites, $10 for rustic and $8 for walk-in sites. In the past, the campground would fill up only on weekends but this may change since the renovation of the facility. The National Park Service may also start booking site reservations in 1993.

18

BARNES
ANTRIM COUNTY PARK

Region: Northwest
Nearest Community: Eastport
Sites: 35   **Reservations:** No
Fee: $10
Information: Park office (616) 599-2712

The highest speed bumps I've ever driven across are in Barnes County Park. They're so high they mark them on the park map and if you go over one faster than 5 mph you're likely to leave your trailer behind. But they're simply an indication of the quiet and family-orientated nature of this 120-acre Antrim County park.

Barnes Park, half hidden near Eastport, is an extremely clean and well maintained facility featuring both rustic and modern campgrounds. It lacks boating facilities, hiking trails and opportunities for anglers but what a beach along scenic Grand Traverse Bay, the reason this campground is filled during the summer.

Directions: The park is 24 miles north of Traverse City along US-31. At the junction of US-31 and M-88, turn west and head a half mile towards the bay where the campground entrance is posted.

Campground: Barnes is a single loop of 60 sites and a mixED bag as far as campgrounds are concerned. Half of the sites, 1-35 located along the east side of the loop, are modern with electric and water hook-ups. The other 25, numbers 51-76, are on the west side and rustic. There is a modern restroom with showers and a dumping station nearby on one half of the loop, and vault toilets for the rustic sites on the other half. All sites have a table and either a pedestal grill or a fire ring.

Sites range from secluded spots in a heavy forest of hardwoods to a few near the open day-use area. Many are close together, some are well secluded including a few modern sites. Rustic sites, 60-66, are located on the edge of the bluff above Lake Michigan but these nor any others have a clear view through the trees of Grand Traverse Bay.

Day-use Facilities: Two shelters, picnic tables and pedestal grills are located in a shady area as you enter the campground. The center of the loop is an open grassy area featuring a variety of play equipment and even a basketball court and a volleyball net.

Next to site 66 is parking for a handful of cars and next to site 57 is changing shelter for swimmers. From either one you can access the bay. The beach is wide, sandy and beautiful. To the north you can spot a few cottages but to the south it's nothing but sand and surf as the park includes more than a quarter mile of lakeshore. The swimming in the bay's clear water and sandy bottom is excellent.

Season: Barnes is open from mid-May through mid-October. In July through August it's often filled on the weekends even though there are some overfilled sites available. No reservations are accepted and generally you can obtain a site Sunday through Wednesday. There is no fee for day-use of the beach.

19 PETOSKEY STATE PARK

Region: The Tip
Nearest Community: Petoskey
Sites: 190 **Reservations:** Yes
Fee: $13 plus vehicle entry permit
Information: Park headquarters (616) 347-2311

In that commercialized shoreline that is Little Traverse Bay there is one haven from the strip of hotels, marinas and condominiums that begins in Petoskey and doesn't quit until you leave Harbor Springs. That 300-acre sanctuary is Petoskey State Park that lies between the two tourist towns.

The state park may not be large but it's amazing what it offers; some of the most secluded modern sites in the state, a beautiful beach, good hunting for Petoskey stones, even some short hiking trails. Needless to say such a facility in a tourist area is going to be filled throughout much of the summer despite it's two large campgrounds.

Directions: The park is 4.5 miles north of downtown Petoskey. Follow US-31 to M-119 and then north (left) for 1.5 miles to the posted entrance.

Campgrounds: The park has 190 sites divided between two campground loops. The *Dunes Campground* is the original facility and has modern sites in a forested area of low dunes. For as

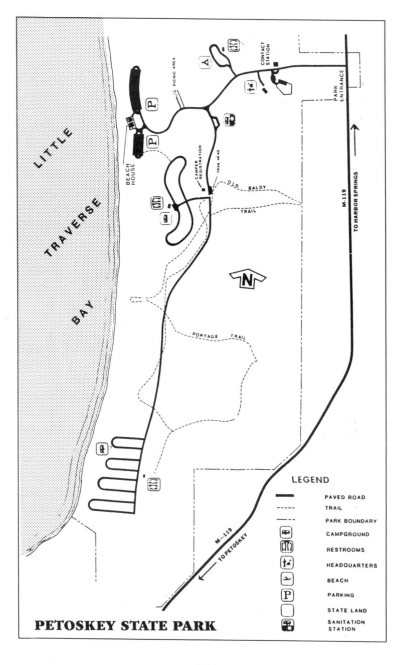

PETOSKEY STATE PARK

close as they are to each other, these sites are as secluded as any modern campground you'll find in a state park. The area is heavily forested and the terrain of rolling dunes allows most of the sites to occupy a little nook of their own. Along the backside of the loop, the foredunes are actually pouring into some of the campsites and from here it's only a short walk to the beach. The loop is paved but not the spurs and large RVs might have difficulty with some of the sites.

Tannery Creek Campground is at the south end of the park and consists of four loops of 100 sites in a level, lightly forested area. Tannery Creek lacks that charming seclusion of the Dunes, especially the final loop where many of the sites have no shade at all. Four wooden walkways provide access to Little Traverse Bay and at this end the beach is a mixture of sand and pebbles, dismaying to swimmers but a paradise for petoskey stone hunters. Both loops have restrooms with showers, sanitation stations, firewood bins and tables and grills at each site.

Day-use Facilities: At the north end of the park is shaded picnic area with tables and pedestal grills and the entrance to group campsites. Nearby on the Bay is the beach and a marked swimming area. Here the shoreline is sandy, wide and enclosed by several dunes. There is a bathhouse/concession store and two parking lots that hold 300 vehicles. The view of the bay is pleasant as you look out over the entire body of water that is often dotted by the colorful spinnakers of sailboats.

Hiking: *Old Baldy Trail* is a 0.75-mile loop that begins with a staircase across from the camper registration station near Dunes Campground. It's an uphill climb in the first half where at one point you come to a bench and a partial view of Little Traverse Bay at the top of a staircase. That's it for the view, there is none on top unless it's fall. The return is a wild romp down a soft sandy path back to the station.

Portage Trail has trailheads near the Tannery Creek restroom and the firewood bin at Dunes campground. Much of it runs parallel to the park drive and is a better ski trail in the winter than a hiker's path during the summer. But it does swing east of the road into a forested area of some surprisingly steep hills.

Season: The campground is open from mid-April to mid-October and fills up most weekends from June through Labor Day and daily from July through mid-August. The park reserves 70 percent of its sites out and Fourth of July weekend is usually booked by April 1. Call the park headquarters for reservations two months in advance for a July or August weekend.

20 HOEFT STATE PARK

Region: The Tip
Nearest Community: Rogers City
Sites: 144   **Reservations:** Yes
Fee: $10 plus vehicle entry permit
Information: Park headquarters (517) 734-2543

In 1922, Paul H. Hoeft, who had spent most of his adult life chopping trees down in Michigan, gave the state 300 timbered acres along Lake Huron. The lumber baron's gift soon became a popular camping area and one of Michigan's original state parks.

Not much has changed since. With few exceptions, the original acreage and boundaries have remain intact. And despite drawing less than 70,000 visitors a year, most of them are campers who can easily fill the 144 sites on any weekend in July and August.

The popularity of Hoeft is easy to understand. The park has a beautiful beach, a series of low dunes for children to climb, a nice network of trails and, if you're an early morning riser, some of the best sunrises in Michigan. Best of all, it rarely seems overrun like so many state parks along Lake Michigan.

Directions: The park is 5 miles northwest of Rogers City with an entrance on US-23.

Campground: The modern campground has 144 well spread out sites along several loops in a stand of hemlock and pine. There are 15 sites that border the low dunes and provide quick access to the Lake Huron beach. Site 35, though not along the dunes, might be the most secluded modern one in the Lower Peninsula while a few near the road are in a semi-open area.

Along with two shower/restroom buildings, tables and fire rings, the campground features a small store, horseshoe pits, limited play equipment and a firewood bin where timber is sold from 6:30 to 8:30 p.m. daily during the summer. There is also a handicapped access site and four Rent-A-Tents, wall tents on wooden platforms that can be rented.

Day-use Facility: Hoeft's shoreline is a mile of wide sandy beach, ideal for beachcombing or setting up a lawn chair to watch freighters sail

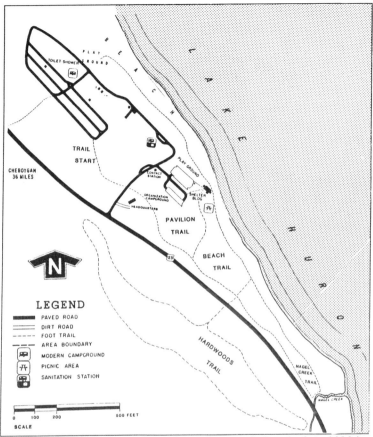

by. The day-use area has a classic log and stone shelter, built in 1938 by the Civilian Conservation Corps, that can be rented in advance along with additional play equipment, tables and grills well separated in a stand of pines. There is also a marked swimming area near the campground.

Fishing: Annual plantings of salmon, lake and brown trout off Rogers City has resulted in a strong deepwater fishery within a mile of the Lake Huron shoreline. There is no ramp in the park, but there are launching facilities in both Rogers City and Hammond Bay. The only fishing in the park is at Nagel Creek, which occasionally attracts river anglers in the fall for spawning salmon and steelhead trout.

Hiking: The park has a 4.5-mile network of foot paths that centers around the *Beach Trail*. This 1.2-mile loop begins between sites 21 and 23 and passes through the low dunes before returning through the park's wooded interior. At its east end the *Hardwood Trail* heads south, crosses US-23 and then forms a 1.4-mile loop through a forest of oak, maple and beech. Also extending from the east end of the Beach Trail is *Nagel Creek Trail*, which forms a 0.75-mile loop to the small creek.

Season: The campground is open May to December and in the late fall electricity and pump water are still available but vault toilets replace the restrooms. Hoeft often fills up on the weekends in July and August and occasionally during the week in mid-August. Call the park headquarters for reservations.

21 ONAWAY STATE PARK

Region: The Tip
Nearest Community: Onaway
Sites: 101   **Reservations:** Yes
Fee: $10 plus a vehicle entry fee
Information: Park headquarters (517) 733-8279

The perception of state parks by many is a campground where the sites are close together and fill for much of the summer. That's true in some units but not Onaway State Park on the south end of Black Lake.

The rollling 158-acre unit is well forested in white pine, maple, oak, attracts an army of morel mushroom every spring and contains almost a mile of shoreline. But the park's most attractive features is that it draws less than 60,000 visitors a year and that a "No Vacancy" sign is rarely seen here, even on a weekend.

Directions: From I-75, depart east at exit 310 and follow M-68 to the town of Onaway. Turn north on M-211 and follow it six miles to it's end at the park entrance.

Campground: Onaway has 101 sites well scattered on a hillside loop that is lightly forested by towering red and white pine. There are no sites directly on the lake but most of them lie uphill from the shore and have a view of the water. Sites have tables and fire rings while a restroom with showers and a sanitation station is located within the loop.

Day-use Facilities: There is a picnic area on the east side of the park that includes tables, grills, a shelter that can be rented and parking

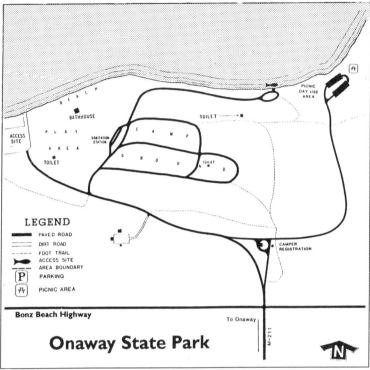

LEGEND

▬▬▬ PAVED ROAD
═══ DIRT ROAD
----- FOOT TRAIL
🐟 ACCESS SITE
AREA BOUNDARY
[P] PARKING
[🏕] PICNIC AREA

Bonz Beach Highway

To Onaway

M-211

Onaway State Park

for 75 cars. But there is no beach and that's the major drawback of Onaway. The only sand is on the west side of the campground and it's a very narrow strip at best. Limited play equipment is located here.

Fishing: Black Lake is the eighth largest in the state, measuring 6 miles in length, 4 miles wide and containing 10,130 surface acres. It's a beautiful body of water and regarded by many as one of the finest walleye fisheries in Michigan. The popularity of fishing on Black Lake prompted the Onaway staff to recently rebuild an improved boat launch west of the campground.

Black Lake also boasts self-sustaining populations of Great Lakes muskies, northern pike and perch. The rocky shore and points, while not too attractive to swimmers and sunbathers, draws a number of shore anglers to try their luck with long casts.

Season: The campground is open from May through to mid-October and generally only fills on Fourth of July and one or two other weekends during summer.

22 LAKESHORE
WILDERNESS STATE PARK

Region: The Tip
Nearest Community: Mackinaw City
Sites: 150   **Reservations:** Yes
Fee: $13 plus vehicle entry permit
Information: Park headquarters (616) 436-5381

There are two parks in Michigan where you can camp in view of the Mackinac Bridge. One is the Straits State Park in the Upper Peninsula and the other is Wilderness State Park west of Mackinaw City. Of the two... actually there is no comparison between them. Wilderness makes a far more enjoyable camping trip, offering some of the finest beaches at the Tip, an excellent trail network and fishing opportunities for both children and diehard bass anglers.

The 7,514-acre park has two campgrounds. Pines offers 60 sites in a rolling terrain lightly forested in red pine and oaks and Lakeshore Campground is a loop of 150 sites with almost a third of them along Big Stone Bay. Quick access to the beach and the beauty of this historical waterway between the Lower and Upper Peninsula, makes Lakeshore one of the most popular state park facilities.

Directions: The park entrance is 8 miles west of Mackinaw City and is reached by following County Road 81 and continuing west on Wilderness Park Drive after crossing Carp Lake River.

Campground: Lakeshore has two loops of 150 sites in a lightly shaded area overlooking the Straits. Forty sites are along the shoreline, many right above the open beach, others are partly shaded and a short walk from the water. Site 38 is a gem, off by itself in a stand of pines. Throughout the loop there is a nice view of the Straits, the Mighty Mac and the Upper Peninsula shoreline. The shoreline along Big Stone Bay is excellent for swimming or just strolling along its sandy beach. Lakeshore has tables, fire rings, two restrooms with showers, a sanitation station, and play equipment.

Day-use Facilities: The park's picnic area is also on Big Stone Bay, just east of the campground. Here you'll find tables overlooking the

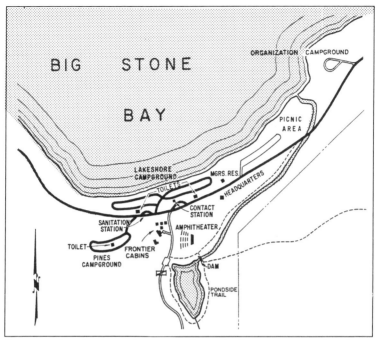

Straits, pedestal grills, vault toilets and a marked swimming area bordered by a sandy beach.

Fishing: The park has an improved launch just west of Lakeshore Campground. But for Wilderness' most noted fishing opportunity, you don't even need a boat. The rocky inlets and pools along Waugoshance Point are a spawning area for smallmouth bass and when the season opens in May anglers don waders to stalk the beds along the north end of Sturgeon Bay. Drive to the end of the park road and from there it's a half mile walk to the first pools along the shoreline. Anglers rig up nightcrawlers or use small spinners such as Mepps or Panther Martins to entice the fish.

Children will find fishing opportunities for bluegill and other panfish in Goose Pond. The fish are stunted but plentiful and the most popular spot to toss in bobbers and bait is off the bridge at the south end of the pond.

Hiking: Wilderness has 12 miles of designated foot trails, most of them resembling two-tracks roads that wander through the backside of the park. But an excellent set of interpretive trails begins at a trailhead on Goose Pond. The *Pondside Trail*, a half-mile walk around the pond,

Father and son display their catch of bass off Waugoshance Point.

begins here along with *Red Pine Trail,* a 1.25-mile walk east to Mt. Nebo Trail. At this point you can continue on the *Hemlock Trail,* a half-mile walk to the remains of an old lookout tower on Mt. Nebo where there is a partial view of the Straits after the leaves drop. Across from the day-use parking area is the posted trailhead for *Big Stone Trail,* which winds past some interesting beaver activity along the creek.

Season: The campgrounds are open year-round and have electricity but the restrooms are closed from Oct. 30 to May 15. During the off-season vault toilets are installed and water is available from the headquarters. There is an off-season rate of $7 per night. During the summer both campgrounds are filled almost daily from July through mid-August. Call the park headquarters for reservations.

RUSTIC
CAMPGROUNDS

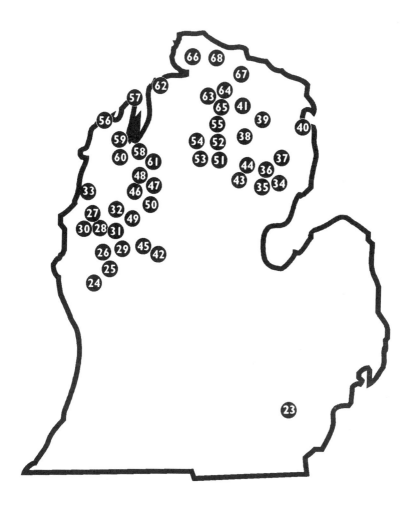

23

CROOKED LAKE
PINCKNEY RECREATION AREA

Region: Southeast
Nearest Community: Pinckney
Sites: 25   **Reservations:** No
Fee: $6 plus a vehicle entry permit
Information: Park headquarters (313) 426-4913

This may be southeast Michigan but the drive to this campground is surprisingly scenic. It begins with North Territorial Road and even though houses are beginning to pop up like mushrooms in the spring it's still a winding avenue past rolling farms and woodlots. Once in the park you follow a narrow dirt road through the hills of this rugged area north of Ann Arbor, reach a highpoint of 1,008 feet and then descend to the lakeshore campground.

Crooked Lake not only combines a sense of being in the woods with a scenic site, but being in Pinckney Recreation Area, a 9994-acre state park unit, it offers a variety of opportunities for hiking, mountain biking, fishing and paddling in a chain of lakes.

Directions: From I-94 depart at exit 159 and head north on M-52 for 6 miles to North Territorial Road and then east. From US-23 north of Ann Arbor depart at exit 49 and turn west onto North Territorial Road for 12 miles. The campground is reached by turning north onto Dexter-Townhall Road from North Territorial and then left on Silver Creek Road to enter the park and drive pass its headquarters. The dirt road ends at Crooked Lake.

Campground: This pleasant campground is situated on a hillside overlooking Crooked Lake. The sites are spread out in a semi-open area partially shaded by pines and large oaks. Only one site, number 7, is directly on the shoreline but most of them have at least a partial view of the water. The sites are well spread out and a few, number 13 in particular, are even off by themselves. Sites have fire rings and tables while located in the loop are vault toilets and a hand pump for water.

Lakeshore campsite at Crooked Lake.

Day-use Facilities: There is no swimming or beach on Crooked Lake. But just down the road is the day-use beach on Silver Lake featuring open grassy area, marked swimming area, tables, pedestal grills, a store and a boat rental concession.

Fishing: Within the campground is an unimproved dirt boat launch while next to it is a handicapped access fishing pier. Children will enjoy the dock but small panfish is all you can expect to catch in water this shallow. Crooked Lake has only a few homes along the shore opposite of the campground while it's south end features a group of small islands. You can follow a channel into Pickerel Lake where at its east end flat bottom boats and canoes can even enter another small lake. Along with panfish, Crooked features bass, northern pike and crappie. Pickerel, which has a fishing pier at its west end, is stocked every spring with rainbow trout.

Hiking: Crossing Silver Lake Road just uphill from the campground is *Crooked Lake Trail,* a 4-mile loop that begins in the Silver Lake Day-use Area. To avoid problems with mountain bikers, hikers are urged to follow the trail in a counter-clockwise direction and in 3 miles will cross a foot bridge over the channel between Crooked and Pickerel lakes.

Mountain Biking: The trail is also a popular route for mountain bikers who must follow it in a clockwise position. Traveling in this direction, bikers will reach Silver Lake Day-Use area in a mile.

Season: The rustic campground is serviced May though October. Crooked Lake tends to fill up on the weekends from late June through early August but usually there are open sites in mid-week.

24

PINES POINT
MANISTEE NATIONAL FOREST

Region: Lake Michigan
Nearest Community: Hesperia
Sites: 33   **Reservations:** No
Fee: $8
Information: White Cloud Ranger (616) 689-6696

In many ways, Pines Point is your typical national forest campground. It's rustic with vault toilets, hand pumps for water and well spread out, wooded sites. Your typical national forest campground with one exception. Pines Point has a tuber's loop where people can float the South Branch of the White River in an inner tube, ending where they began; in the campground.

There are opportunities to fish, hike, even go backpacking but what most campers enjoy best about this Manistee National Forest facility is spending a hot afternoon cooling off in the gin-clear waters of the White River and never worry about special transportation or arranging a drop-off that tubers must do in other rivers.

Directions: From White Cloud head west on M-20 to Hesperia where you turn south on Maple Island Road. In a mile turn west on Garfield Road for five miles and then south on 168th Avenue where the campground is posted. Follow the blacktop for 2.5 miles to the campground.

Campground: Pines Point has 33 sites spread out on a paved loop on a high bluff above the South Branch of the White River. The area is heavily forested and the sites are well spread out and secluded from each other. Ten sites are on the edge of the bluff with a view of the river and log stairways nearby that lead down the steep shoreline to the water.

The gravelled parking spurs makes this facility ideal for large RVs while other facilities include fire rings with sliding grills, tables, drinking fountains and a flush toilet along with vault toilets.

Day-Use Facilities: A picnic area is situated in a grove of red pine

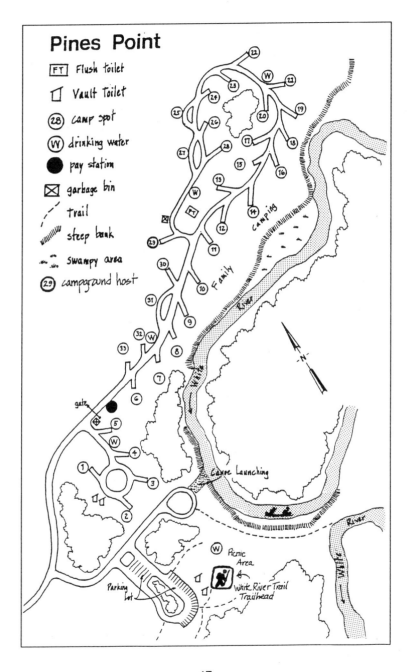

Pines Point

FT Flush toilet

▢ Vault Toilet

(28) camp spot

(W) drinking water

● pay station

⊠ garbage bin

/ / Trail

〜〜〜 steep bank

... swampy area

(29) campground host

Family Camping

White River

White River

gate

Canoe Launching

Picnic Area

White River Trail Trailhead

Parking Lot

N

on the bluff above the water and includes a separate entrance, tables, pedestal grills and a large parking lot. Both the trailhead for the White River Foot Trail and the departure point for tubers is located here. There is $1.50 a day fee to park in the day-use area.

Fishing: The White River is the southern most major trout stream draining into Lake Michigan. At Pines Point you'll find fall and spring steelhead fishing as well as fall salmon which is extremely popular among anglers. White River Trail can also be used to access more remote sections of the river. Other species caught during the summer include smallmouth bass and northern pike.

Tubing: The South Branch of the White River forms an oxbow at Pines Point Campground where tubers can put in at the canoe launch and then get out at the picnic area for a 30- to 40-minute float. This far upstream the South Branch is an ideal waterway for novice tubers. It's 20 to 30 yards wide and so shallow in many stretches even children can stand up.

Canoeing: Pines Point has a canoe landing along the South Branch with boat racks and a pull-through drive for vehicles. Designated "Country Scenic River" by the state, the White River flows through primarily wooded and agriculture land. Most paddlers begin in the town of Hesperia and from there it's a 6-mile, two-hour paddle to the campground. The next take-out is Sischo Bayou, a 7-mile, three-hour journey, while Whiteall on White Lake is a 27-mile paddle from Pines Point. Canoes and transportation can be arranged through *Happy Mohawk Canoe Livery* (616-894-4209).

Hiking: Departing from the day-use area is *White River Trail*, a trail system that is currently being developed by the U.S. Forest Service. Currently there is 12 miles of developed paths marked by blue blazes. The first 2 miles of the trail follows the high banks overlooking the river much of the way and comes to a forest road that can be followed for the trek back. There is also a posted trail to Knapp Lake, a small shallow lake in the middle of the White River Foot Travel Area.

Season: Pines Point has a campground manager that collects fees from Memorial Day through Labor Day and possibly earlier if there is a demand. It's rarely filled in mid-week and only full on holidays and an occasional weekend.

25

BENTON LAKE
MANISTEE NATIONAL FOREST

Region: Lake Michigan
Nearest Community: Brohman
Sites: 24   **Reservations:** No
Fee: $8
Information: White Cloud Ranger (616) 689-6696

What was a turkey farm in the 1940s is now a lightly used campground in the White Cloud District of the Huron-Manistee National Forest. Benton Lake is a mid-size facility of 24 sites located on the south shore of this 33-acre lake. Half of the sites are in the wooded area but the other half are in an open, grassy area, remnants of the poultry farm here.

The farm also had a profound effect on the lake itself. Until the 1950s, Benton Lake was private water that was rarely fished and that, say some locals, is the reason for the Benton Lake's excellent bluegill fishery.

Directions: The campground is an hour drive north of Grand Rapids. From M-37 in Brohman turn west on Pierce Drive (also labeled Forest Road 5308) and drive 4.5 miles to the posted entrance of the campground.

Campground: There are 24 sites on two loops with sites 1-12 located in an area forested in young hardwoods with moderate undergrowth. Much of the second loop is open, however, and the grassy sites are closer to the lakes. There are none directly on the water but several are only a few steps away. Sites feature a table, fire ring with sliding grill, lantern post and paved spurs, making them ideal for RVs. Both loops have vault toilets and hand pumps for water.

Day-use Facilities: The campground has a pleasant picnic area with some of the tables and grills on a grassy hillside overlooking the lake. Although a beach and swimming area is marked on handouts, it's little more than a small clearing in the aquatic vegetation, just enough for young children. There is additional parking and a vault toilet at the picnic area.

Fishing: Beyond the picnic area is an unimproved boat launch on the northwest corner of the lake. Benton is a 33-acre lake that lies completely

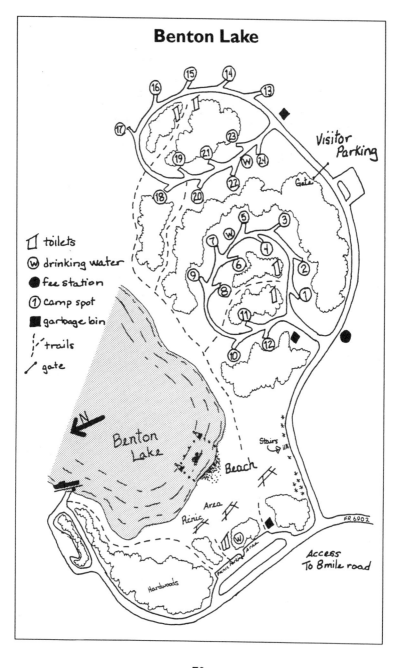

Benton Lake

toilets
drinking water
fee station
camp spot
garbage bin
trails
gate

N

Benton Lake

Beach

Stairs

Picnic Area

Hardwoods

Visitor Parking

Gate

Access To 8mile road

FR 6902

A rustic site at Benton Lake Campground.

in national forest land thus free of any cottages or other development. It's not large and attracts only light fishing pressure throughout most of the summer. There is a drop-off 15 to 20 yards off shore and during the summer anglers who fish the edge of it with wax and leaf worms can often entice a variety of panfish. Some bluegills that have come out of the lake have easily exceeded a pound.

Hiking: There is a trailhead for the *North Country Trail* located off Pierce Drive, 2 miles east of the campground entrance. To the north along the NCT it's approximately a 4- to 5-mile trek to Nichols Lake Campground (see page 72), to the south a 3- to 4-mile hike to Loda Lake Wildflower Sanctuary.

Season: The campground is managed by a concessionaire from Memorial Day to Labor Day. Sites are occupied on a first-come-first-serve basis and have a capacity of eight people and two vehicles.

26

NICHOLS LAKE
MANISTEE NATIONAL FOREST

Region: Lake Michigan
Nearest Community: Woodland Park
Sites: 28   **Reservations:** No
Fee: $8
Information: White Cloud Ranger (616) 689-6696

Of the eight National Forest campgrounds located between White Cloud and Baldwin, Nicholas Lake is one of the most poplar because it's one of the nicest. Overlooking a scenic lake, the facility is well wooded with well spread out sites and paved spurs. You can sneak off into the woods on the North Country Trail, fish for bluegill in Nicholas Lake or trailer your boat to dozens of other lakes in the area.

Little wonder then that this facility is often filled on a summer weekend. No reservations are accepted but Nicholas Lake is well worth arriving a day early to beat the Friday night crowd.

Directions: From White Cloud, head north on M-37 for 13 miles and then turn west on 11 Mile Road. The posted entrance of the campground is reached in 4.5 miles or 3 miles beyond the community of Woodland.

Campground: Nicholas Lake is a single loop of 28 sites situated on a bluff wooded predominantly by oaks. Sites are well spread out but within sight of each other due to thin undergrowth. One side of the bluff borders the lake and a few sites have a partial view of the water. On the other side several sites overlook a grassy marsh, an excellent area to watch for deer in the early evening.

Sites include not only fire rings with sliding grills and tables but also lantern posts. Within the loop are both vault and flush toilets and three spigots for water. The other nice aspect about Nicholas Lake is the bluff catches any breeze at all on the lake, making the campground a little less bug infested during the summer.

Day-use Facilities: A path next to site number 17 leads down the

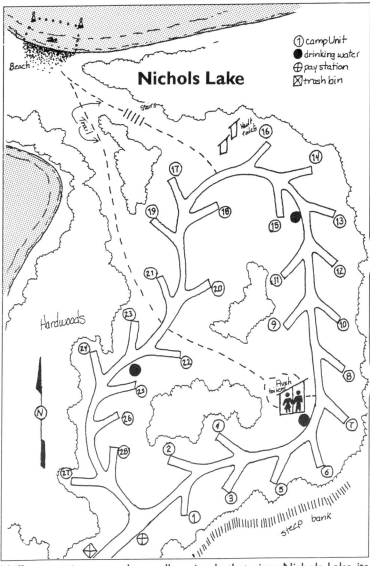

Nichols Lake

Beach

① camp Unit
● drinking water
⊕ pay station
☒ trash bin

Hardwoods

Vault toilets

Flush toilets

steep bank

bluff via a staircase to the small peninsula that gives Nichols Lake its horseshoe shape. At the base of the point is small strip of sand with a posted swimming area. From here the path climbs to the end of the point for a nice overview of the entire lake and who's fishing where.

On the northwest corner of the lake is a separate picnic area with tables and pedestal grills that is reached from Cleveland Road via Bitely. The North Country Trail connects the area with the campground.

Fishing: Before entering the campground you pass a separate spur that leads to the trailhead for the North Country Trail and an improved boat launch. There are parking areas for both here. Nichols Lake has a 160 surface acres and is horse-shaped with cottages and developed shoreline limited almost entirely to the northeast corner. The prime species are bluegills and the lake receives moderate fishing pressure throughout the summer.

Anglers who enjoy hike-in fishing experiences can follow the North Country Trail to the north to reach isolated Leaf Lake in two miles.

Hiking: The *North Country Trail* passes through the campground and has a trailhead near the boat launch. The most scenic section by far is to head north to pass through Nichols Lake Picnic Area and across Cleveland Road. In the next three miles the trail winds past five lakes.

Season: The managed season is from Memorial Day to Labor Day but call the White Cloud Ranger District for exact opening dates. If arriving on a Friday or Saturday afternoon be prepared for the possibility of this campground being filled.

27

DRIFTWOOD VALLEY
MANISTEE NATIONAL FOREST

Region: Lake Michigan
Nearest Community: Irons
Sites: 21   **Reservations:** No
Fee: $5
Information: Manistee Ranger (616) 723-2211

The Little Manistee River is among the best known steelhead waters in the state. During the month of April the river is alive with both fish spawning upstream and anglers who toss spinners, plugs and spawn in an effort to entice the hard-fighting rainbows into striking. Of the three national forest campgrounds located along the river, the Bear Track facility downstream offers better canoeing along with hiking opportuni-

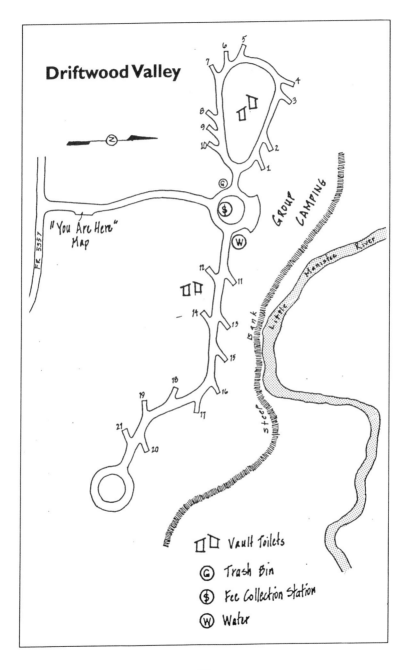

Driftwood Valley

"You Are Here" Map

Group CAMPING

Little Manistee River

steep Bank

FR 5357

🔲🔳 Vault Toilets

Ⓖ Trash Bin

Ⓢ Fee Collection Station

Ⓦ Water

ties on the North Country Trail that passes nearby.

But Driftwood Valley makes a more scenic place to camp, especially in the fall when river fishermen do well working this stretch of the Little Manistee. Canoeing is possible downstream from the campground but upriver the paddling is a challenge due to shallow water and overhanging brush.

Directions: From Wellston depart M-55 south on Bosschem Road (also labeled County Road 669) for 4 miles and then west (right) on 12 Mile Road for a half mile and south (left) on Bass Road for 4 miles where the road curves between Elbow and Harper Lake. Beyond the lakes turn west (right) on Forest Road 5357 and the posted entrance is less than a mile.

Campground: Driftwood Valley is a pair of loops on a high bank above the river. The area is forested in white pine and oaks and the 21 sites well separated from each other. Although none are directly on the water, five of them are on the edge of the bluff from which you can look down at the Little Manistee gurgling past you. Amenities include vault toilets, hand pumps for water, fire ring with sliding grill and a group camping area for paddlers between the two loops.

Fishing: The river is best known by river anglers as a steelhead stream and fished hard in April. But Chinook and coho salmon can also be caught, primarily from October through November, and to a lesser degree brown trout. There are no official trails in the area but an angler's path runs along much of the river from the campground.

Canoeing: There is a carry-down canoe launch located adjacent to the group campsite. The Little Manistee is not nearly as popular as the Pere Marquette or the Pine but still makes for enjoyable paddling. M-37 is the upper limit for canoeists and from there the river winds 85 miles to Manistee Lake near Lake Michigan. From Driftwood it's a 2-hour paddle to Bear Track Campground, which also has a canoe launch. The next landing is Nine Mile Bridge, a 5-hour paddle from Driftwood. Canoes are rented in Wellston from *Jarolim Canoes* (616) 862-3475.

Season: The managed season for the campground is Memorial Day through Labor Day and except during the spring steelhead runs, Driftwood is a lightly used facility.

28

HIGHBANK LAKE
MANISTEE NATIONAL FOREST

Region: Lake Michigan
Nearest Community: Baldwin
Sites: 9   **Reservations:** No
Fee: $8
Information: Baldwin Ranger (616) 745-4631

Highbank Lake is well named. It is indeed encircled by bluffs, forested in hardwoods and towering above the water. Add the fact that the entire lake lies in the Manistee National Forest and you have the reasons why this small campground is a somewhat remote and secluded but a charming place to spend a night or even longer.

There are a couple of cottages along the southeast corner of the lake, but they're tucked way up on the shoreline bluff and not obtrusive at all. Nor does the lake buzz with motor boats or water skiers. Small at 20 acres, Highbank Lake has only a unimproved boat launch at the campground. Anything bigger than a hand-carried rowboat and you're going to have problems launching it.

Fishing opportunities abound in the area and the North Country Trail swings nearby and can be reached by the adventurous trekker. But be forewarned, with only nine sites this facility is filled most weekends from mid-June through Labor Day and often during the middle of the week.

Directions: To reach the campground from US-10 in Baldwin head south on M-37 for 9 miles to the junction of 16 Mile Road in Lilley. Turn west on 16 Mile Road for a half mile then north (right) on Roosevelt Drive where the campground is posted. The lake is reached 1.5 miles up Roosevelt Drive. From the south, 16 Mile Road is 17 miles from White Cloud.

Campground: Highbank Lake campground is a single loop of nine sites. There are hard gravelled parking spurs on seven of them of which four allow you to park the recreational vehicle within a few yards of the water. Two other sites are labeled "walk-in" and the site is actually located up a short staircase from where you park the car. Vault toilets and a hand pump for water rounds out the facilities while sites have tables and fire rings with sliding grills.

Day-Use Facilities: Forest Service handouts show a beach near site number 3 but in reality it's a grassy bank leading down to the lake's sandy bottom where children can spend a hot afternoon splashing away. Two benches are located here and angled in such a way that you can catch the sun dipping behind the a shoreline bluff in the evening or watch fishermen enticing bluegills with worms and crickets.

Fishing: Near the beach you can launch a hand-carried boat and canoes are perfect for this 20-acre lake. Panfish, most notably bluegill, and bass are the species most anglers are targeting here. Shore fishermen can follow a foot path along the shore at the east end of the lake and this little inlet can be especially productive when bluegills are spawning in May.

For a little angling adventure try fishing Amaung Lake. The lake lies due east of Highbank but there is no ramp on it or even a road to it. Follow Roosevelt Drive (also Forest Road 5396) past the entrance of the campground for another quarter mile and then just head into the woods. The lake is only a few hundred yards away and it's hard to miss, it is considerably larger than Highbank. Amaung offers less fishing pressure and seems to have a better population of largemouth bass as well as panfish. Haul a canoe or belly boat in and it could be a rewarding afternoon for the extra effort.

Hiking: There are no designated trails from the campground but traversing along the bluff that borders the west side of the lake is the *North Country Trail*. This is one of the best scenic stretches of the Baldwin Segment of the NCT. North of Highbank is a small lake that can be reached only on foot while to the south the trail winds around Condon and Leaf Lakes before reaching a trailhead on Cleveland Road. From its perch over Highbank Lake to Cleveland Road is a trek of 3.5 miles. To reach the trail, follow the anglers trail around the east side of the lake and then climb to the top of the west shore bluff. On the bluff the trail is a well beaten path marked by blue diamonds.

Season: The managed season is from Memorial Day through Labor Day but if spring weather is warm the concessionaire will begin collecting fees earlier. The campground often fills on weekends. If you want a site here plan on arriving early in the day and have an alternative campground picked out...just in case.

29

SHELLEY LAKE
MANISTEE NATIONAL FOREST

Region: Heartland
Nearest Community: Brohman
Sites: 9   **Reservations:** No
Fees: None
Information: White Cloud Ranger (616) 689-6696.

Spending a night at Shelley Lake in Manistee National Forest is something that falls between hiking in and pulling up to your site with a car full of coolers, lawn chairs and a deluxe, three-burner Coleman stove. The U.S. Forest Service calls it a "dispersed recreation area" which means it's non-developed; no toilets, no fire rings, no facilities what-so-ever.

It means you're out in the woods and off by yourself, all by careful design.

The recreation area was set up after unrestricted use of the scenic area began causing irreversible damage to the small, 15-acre lake. So barriers were built across the old logging roads leading up to the shoreline and nine campsites were designated.

You can pull right up to a couple of the campsites away from the lake. But the best ones are along the shoreline, overlooking the water, and those you have park and walk to. Not

A Shelley Lake camper.

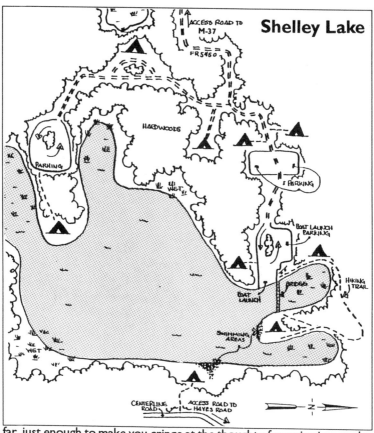

far, just enough to make you cringe at the thought of carrying in a cooler full of ice and soda pop.

Directions: From White Cloud head north on M-37 and then turn east on a primitive, unposted road just before passing 11 Mile Road. Access to the area is by a very rough forest road not recommended for large recreation vehicles while some sites are reached on foot from a parking area.

Campground: The facility has nine designated sites around the small lake and you have to walk into seven of them. One is on a point in the southwest corner where you pitched the tent in a stand of paper birch with a 180-degree view of the water. At the north end of the lake is a site reached via a foot bridge across a small inlet. Another is on the east side reached from M-37 by heading east on Hayes Road and then south on

Centerline Road. From a parking area on Centerline it's a quarter-mile walk through the forest where you break out at a small sandy beach. There are no tables, fire rings, vault toilets or safe water source within the campground.

Fishing: At the north end of the lake there is an unimproved boat launch onto the lake and parking for two maybe three vehicles. The 15-acre lake is completely surrounded by national forest land and can be fished for both bluegill and other species of panfish as well as bass. The fishing pressure on Shelley is generally light.

Season: The managed season is Memorial Day through Labor Day but camping is allowed year-round. Keep in mind this campground is hard to reach during spring and late fall or after any extended period of rain.

30

SAND LAKE
MANISTEE NATIONAL FOREST

Region: Lake Michigan
Nearest Community: Dublin
Sites: 45   **Reservations:** Yes
Fee: $8
Information: Manistee Ranger (616) 723-2211

Vault toilets get you down? So do modern campgrounds with their crowded sites? Sand Lake in the Manistee National Forest is an excellent comprise. Sites here are well spread out in a heavily forested area. Some are even off by themselves.

Yet at this national forest facility you can reserve a site in advance, though it is usually not necessary, not even on most weekends. Best of all for some people, Sand Lake has flush toilets as well as old fashion vault toilets. Sometimes that's all you need to get mom to go camping.

Directions: From M-55 head to Wellston and then turn south on Seaman Road. Follow the road 4.5 miles as it passes through the village of Dublin. A mile south of Dublin, turn west on Forest Service Road 5728 where the campground is posted.

Campground: Sand Lake has three loops of 45 sites with tables, fire

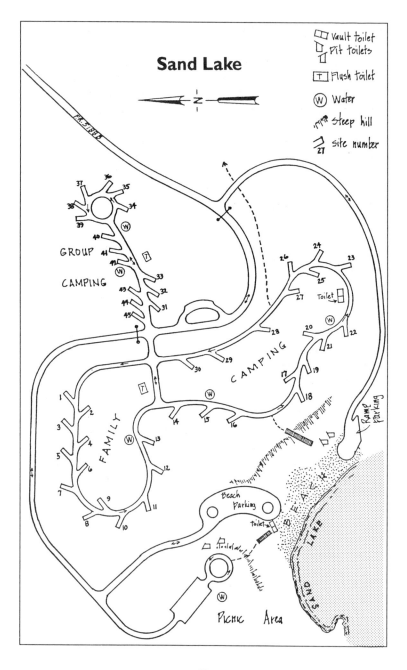

Sand Lake

rings with sliding grills and paved spurs. The loops with sites 1 through 30 on them are in a hilly area forested in a variety of hardwoods. The sites here are well separated and some totally off by themselves without a neighbor in view. There are none directly on Sand Lake but a handful (sites 16-19) are conveniently located next to a stairway that leads directly to campground's beach. Other facilities on the loops include flush toilets, vault toilets and spigots for water.

Day-use Facilities: The campground has a beautiful and very wide beach with a marked swimming area, bathhouse and separate parking lot. During the summer a lifeguard arrives at 11 a.m. Located on a bluff overlooking the beach is a small picnic area with tables and grills. The campground managers charge $1 per adult and 50 cents per child as a day use fee to non-campers.

Fishing: The campground has a ramp area for carry-in boats only with additional parking for anglers but it's $3 for non-campers to launch. Canoes and rowboats are available for rent during the summer.

Sand Lake has 50 surface acres and a shoreline that, except for the small portion in the campground, is privately owned. There are many cottages yet the lake doesn't appear to be as developed as many further south. Sand Lake's fishery is a mixed bag. It's stocked with rainbow trout but many anglers target it for bass while other are just happy to catch a few perch or bluegill.

Hiking: There's a short nature trail that is less than a mile long and begins across from site 28. It has 12 interpretive posts but you might be hard pressed to find the corresponding guide.

Season: The campground is managed from Memorial Day through Labor Day. Reservations can be made by calling the hosts at (616) 848-4349 though it's rarely full in the middle of the week and open sites exist even on most weekends. Check with the Manistee Ranger District if the reservation number is changed.

31

BOWMAN BRIDGE
MANISTEE NATIONAL FOREST

Region: Lake Michigan
Nearest Community: Baldwin
Sites: 20   **Reservations:** No
Fee: $6
Information: Baldwin Ranger (616) 745-4631

Location and quick access is the nicest aspect of this national forest campground located just west of Baldwin. Bowman Bridge lies on the banks of the Pere Marquette, a National Scenic River and a very popular destination with canoers during the summer as evident by the number of group campsites found here.

But also within the campground is a foot path that connects it to the North Country Trail and the Bowman Lake Foot Travel Area, both excellent areas for hikers and backpackers to explore. The rustic facility lacks the solitude and privacy of many others in the national forest, especially when it's filled, but at this campground it's easy to wander off into the woods or paddle up the river to escape the crowds.

Directions: From the junction of US-10 and M-37 head south through downtown Baldwin and in less than a half mile, right before you pass the US Forest Service office, turn west (right) on Seventh Street. In 0.4 miles swing south (left) on Cherry Street and then immediately west (right) on 52nd Street. This road merges into 56th Street and 4.3 miles from Baldwin you cross the Pere Marquette River and pass the posted entrance to the campground.

Campground: Bowman Bridge has 16 sites with paved spurs, four group sites designed primarily for the canoers and four walk-in sites for tent campers. All are located on two loops along a bluff above the river in an area lightly forested in maples and oaks with thin undergrowth. Facilities include hand pumps, tables, fire rings with grills and vault toilets.

Canoeing: A large canoe launch is featured below the campground with a paved pull-through, racks and parking lot. There is even additional parking on the other side of 56th Street, that's how popular a pull-out at

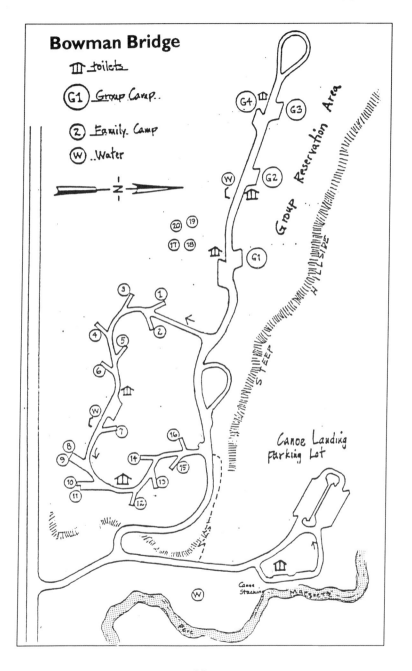

Bowman Bridge is for paddlers.

The Pere Marquette is the only free-flowing river in the Lower Peninsula without any impoundments and for most canoeists its an exhilarating paddle. A free permit is required for all watercraft on the river from May 15 to Sept. 10. If you rent a canoe, the livery will provide a permit, if you use your own, pick one up from the Forest Service office in Baldwin.

Canoers can paddle 66 miles of the river. From M-37 in Baldwin, it's a 12-mile, four-hour paddle to Bowman Bridge. The next take out is Rainbow Rapids, almost nine miles or two hours down stream. You can obtain rentals in Baldwin from either *Ivan's Canoe Rental* (616-745-3361) or *Baldwin Canoe Rentals* (616-745-4669).

Fishing: Bowman Bridge is the start of the "flies only" stretch of the Pere Marquette which extends 8.7 miles down stream to Rainbow Rapids. Heaviest use of the river by anglers is at the peak of the salmon spawning run in September and October and the height of the steelhead run in March through mid-April. The river also supports brown trout, though many feel this fishery has diminished at the expense of the salmon. Almost a dozen driftboat guides work the Pere Marquette with many of them based in Baldwin.

Hiking: Along the group loop is a trailhead a half-mile spur that is marked in blue diamonds and leads to the *North Country Trail.* On the NCT you can head north and in a mile reach the *Bowman Lake Foot Travel Area.* Bowman Lake is a 1,000-acre non-motorized preserve with a 2.2-mile pathway that circles the scenic lake. You can spend an hour hiking this area or carry in a fishing rod and some bait and spend an afternoon catching bluegills from the shore.

Season: The campground is managed from the last day in Saturday in April through Labor Day but may be open earlier---or later---depending on demand. Reservations can be made by calling the Baldwin Ranger District office. Group sites should be reserved in advance and are $40 per site. Due mostly to canoers, Bowman is a popular campground and will often be filled on the weekends and even mid-week at the height of the camping season.

32

PETERSON BRIDGE
MANISTEE NATIONAL FOREST

Region: Lake Michigan
Nearest Community: Wellston
Sites: 26   **Reservations:** No
Fee: $8
Information: Cadillac Ranger (616) 775-8539

In 1925, Gideon Gerhardt stopped along the Pine River to do a little trout fishing but when he waded down stream to his favorite hole he found "No trespassing" signs all around. The incident triggered the Collins Vs Gerhardt case and eventually the Michigan Supreme Court reversed a lower court in ruling that Frank Collins may have owned the land but the river and all streams, lakes and ponds in the state are public waters.

It was a historical decision for all outdoor enthusiasts and today that spot along the Pine River is part of Peterson Bridge Campground. The facility occupies both sides of the blue-ribbon trout stream, with a campground on the south side and a day-use and canoe landing on the north bank. It's a scenic and popular facility, especially with canoers who can be seen paddling the river from June through August. Thanks in no small part to Gideon Gerhardt.

Directions: The campground is right on M-37, 1.5 miles south of M-55 or 21.5 miles north of Baldwin.

Campground: Peterson Bridge has a single loop of 20 sites, well separated and secluded from each other in a mixed forest of hardwoods. Six sites along the back of the loop are enclosed by a towering wooded bluff while others are on the edge of a steep bank that leads down to the river. Number 20 is the only one with a view of the water as it overlooks where the river sweeps past the canoe landing.

Six walk-in group sites are located at the base of the bank along the river and can be reached by a stairway near the fee station though they are used mostly by canoeists. There are both vault toilets and one flush toilet, water spigots, tables and fire rings with sliding grills.

87

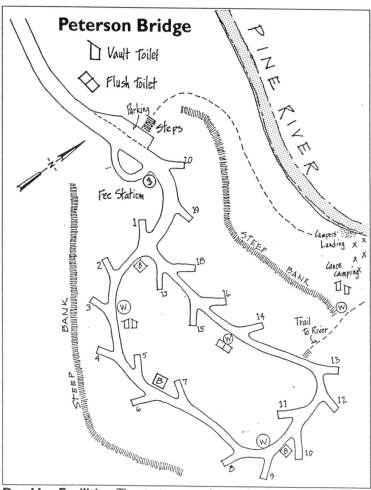

Day-Use Facilities: The picnic area and canoe landing is situated across the river from the campground and is a very pleasant, though often busy, place during the summer. Along with the canoe launch, there are tables and pedestal grills, some overlooking the river, vault toilets, a small shelter, hand pump for water, canoe racks and additional parking for the large number of paddlers that depart from here.

Next to a historical marker dedicated to the famous Michigan Supreme Court case involving the Pine, there is a group of benches in a stand of red pine where undoubtedly more than one tired paddler has sat down, glad that the day on the river is finally over.

Fishing: The Pine is regarded as a high quality trout stream, holding good populations of brown trout this far down stream. The stretch up stream between Walker Bridge and Dobson Bridge was once considered one of the best stretches of water for trout fishermen in the state. To avoid canoers, plan on fishing below Peterson Bridge before noon.

Canoeing: The Pine flows 60 miles from near Leroy until it merges into the Manistee River near Stronach Dam in Manistee County. To paddle the river in national forest land, you need a free permit between May and October and they can be reserved in advance by calling the Permit Station on M-55 at (616) 862-3333. One popular put-in is Elm Flats and it's a 12-mile, four-hour paddle from there to the campground, passing Dobson Bridge along the way. Beyond the campground the final take-out is Low Bridge on M-55, an eight-mile, three-hour journey. Canoes and transportation can be arranged at *Jarolim Canoes* (616-862-3475), *Baldwin Canoes* (616-745-4669) or *Carl's Canoe Livery* (616-797-5156). River hours for paddlers are 9 a.m. to 6 p.m.

Season: The managed season for the campground is Memorial Day through Labor Day and can be filled on any weekend from mid-June through mid-August.

33

LAKE MICHIGAN
MANISTEE NATIONAL FOREST

Region: Lake Michigan
Nearest Community: Manistee
Sites: 100   **Reservations:** Yes
Fee: $7
Information: Manistee Ranger (616) 723-2211

Even though it's a rustic facility, the Lake Michigan Recreation Area is the most popular unit in the national forest and probably one of the most popular campgrounds anywhere in the state regardless who administers it. Located 13 miles south of Manistee on the edge of the Nordhouse Dunes Wilderness, the U.S. Forest facility was once called by Family Circle magazine "one of the 20 best campgrounds in America."

It's easy to understand why.

The beach is beautiful, the dunes provide spectacular vistas, there are great hiking opportunities into the Nordhouse Dunes and just getting to the campground provides a sense of adventure. The recreation area is at the end of Lake Michigan Road (FR 5629), an eight-mile drive from US-31 through nothing but woods. Arrive at dawn or dusk and chances are you'll spot a handful if not a dozen or two of deer along the way.

About the only thing this campground lacks is good fishing opportunities but there are so many other things to do, you won't miss the rod and reel for a few days.

Directions: To reach the campground from Manistee head south on US-31 for 10 miles and then right at Lake Michigan Road. The recreation area is reached in eight miles at the end of the road. If coming from Ludington, Lake Michigan Road is 11.5 miles north of the junction of US-31 and US-10 in Scottville.

Campground: The 100 sites are located on four loops of 25 each with Hemlock and Orchid loops the most popular due to their close proximity to the beach access point and the fact they have flush toilets. The others have vault toilets. The campsites are spacious and well spread out in an area forested in pines and hardwoods, especially oak trees. There is a fire ring, table and a lantern post at each site.

There are no showers but what a beach!

A forested dune separates the sites from Lake Michigan and access to the beach is where Porter Creek empties into the Great Lake. Stone and wood chip paths lead from all the loops to a wooden walkway that serves as entry to a beautiful stretch of golden sand and turquoise surf. If the night is clear you can sit on a bench or the small foredunes and watch a dying sun melt into the dark blue horizon of Lake Michigan.

Day-use Facilities: North of Porter Creek is a day-use area with playground equipment, tables, pedestal grills and two small shelters as well as vault toilets and it's own beach access. Paths and a foot bridge allow campers to cross over and climb the observation deck in the day-use area, one of the two found here. It's 167 steps up to the top of a towering dune but well worth it. From the viewing platform on a clear day you can see miles of beach, acres of dunes and to the south the distinctive black and white tower of the Big Point Sable Lighthouse in Ludington State Park.

Hiking: The second observation deck is reached via a long staircase from the beach walkway near the campground. The view is not nearly as good but located next to the platform is the trailhead for the Nordhouse

The dune overlook at Lake Michigan Recreation Area.

Dunes Wilderness, the only federally-designated wilderness in the Lower Peninsula.

There's a 10-mile network of foot paths in the 3,450-acre preserve, including *Arrowhead Trail,* a 0.8-mile loop that is idea for families with young children. If a child can climb the 122 steps to the observation deck, he or she can handle this short trail. Even better is the route that parallels the shoreline along the crest of a dune. Once referred to as the *Michigan Trail,* this hike is an enchanting walk where you walk while viewing the white sandy beach below or the endless blue of Lake Michigan on the horizon. Return on the first spur back from this trail and it makes for a 2.4-mile loop. Those up for an easy but all-day adventure can hike the beach all the way to the Big Point Sable Lighthouse, a round-trip of eight miles to the historic tower.

Season: The managed season is from Memorial Day through Labor Day but the campground is open year-round unless the access road is closed by snowfall. The facility is often filled from Thursday through Sunday from July 4 through early August. Reservations for sites in the Oak and Orchid loops can be reserved in advance by calling 1-800-283-2267, a national reservation service. There is a reservation fee of $6 and sites must be booked at least 10 days in advance.

34

MONUMENT
HURON NATIONAL FOREST

Region: Lake Huron
Nearest Community: Tawas City
Sites: 20   **Reservations:** No
Fee: $5
Information: Tawas Ranger (517) 362-4477

As a campground, Lumbermen's Monument is only fair, basically 20 sites in a red pine plantation. But the nearby interpretive center, museum, trails and scenic overlooks make this facility an excellent place to spend a weekend. There's much to do at the monument and most of it is only a short walk from the campground.

Directions: From Tawas City head west on M-55 for a mile and then north (right) onto Wilber Road for 1.5 miles to reach Monument Road. Head northwest on Monument Road until it ends at River Road. The entrance to the campground is east (right) on River Road.

Campground: Monument is a single loop in a red pine plantation. The sites are well spread out but, as is typical with pine plantations, there is little undergrowth to isolated one camping party from another. Sites have tables and fire rings with sliding grills while within the loop are vault toilets and spigots for water.

The entrance to the interpretive center is a quarter mile west of the campground but the back of the loop borders the visitor center picnic area and from here a paved path winds past the museum and overlooks.

Day-use Facility: Lumbermen's Monument is an impressive bronze statue of three loggers that was erected in 1931 and today is the center piece of the Huron National Forest's most popular attraction. The interpretive area includes a small museum and outdoor hands-on exhibits devoted to Michigan's logging era at the turn-of-the-century and even a stairway nature trail that explore Michigan's colorful logging area. The overlooks of the AuSable River valley are spectacular in the fall. The visitor center is open daily from 10 a.m. to 7 p.m. through fall colors in mid-October. There is no admission.

Just to the west on River Road is Iargo Springs, another interpretive area where a long stairway leads down the riverside bluff to the fresh water springs that were once a popular resting place for Chippewa Indians on the Saginaw-Mackinac Trail.

Hiking: Crossing the campground's entrance drive and marked in blue diamonds is the *Highbanks Trail*, a seven-mile point-to-point path that extends from Iargo Springs to Sidtown. The trail is named from the fact that it skirts the high bluffs above the AuSable River and along the way you pass many spectacular vistas of the river valley. To the west Iargo Springs is a 3.6-mile walk from the

Lumbermen's Monument

campground and along the way you pass the eagle viewing point in 1.8 miles.

Canoeing: AuSable River is a noted waterway for canoeists (see Keystone Campground page 129), but Monument Campground is not a place to launch a boat due to the steep bluffs.

Season: The campground is managed Memorial Day to Labor Day but may be open earlier or later depending on weather and demand. Lumbermen's Monument is one of the most popular attractions in Huron National Forest and thus the campground is a popular facility, often filled on weekends as early as Thursday evening.

35

ROLLWAYS
HURON NATIONAL FOREST

Region: Lake Huron
Nearest Community: Hale
Sites: 19   **Reservations:** No
Fee: $5
Information: Tawas Ranger (517) 362-4477

Located on high bluffs above the AuSable River, is Rollways National Forest Campground, an alternative if Lumbermen's Monument is full, which it quite often can be. Rollways picks up its name from the turn of the century when lumbermen rolled logs down the steep banks to the river below and then floated them to sawmills on Lake Huron.

You can spend an afternoon learning about Michigan's incredible lumber era at the Monument only eight miles to the east. Then return to camp at Rollways that features the same spectacular panoramas of the AuSable Valley as seen elsewhere along River Road.

Directions: Rollways is posted and located right off M-65 on Rollaway Road. From I-75 depart at exit 188 and take US-23 through Standish and Omer. Two miles out of Omer turn north on M-65, passing through the town Whittemore and Hale. The campground is posted roughly 7 miles north of Hale.

Campground: Rollways is a single loop of 19 sites with paved spurs, tables and fire rings with sliding grills. The campground, lightly forested in large oaks and red pines, is located near the edge of the river bluff. Most sites do not have a clear view of the valley below. The exception is site number 8 where from your picnic table there is incredible overlook of the river below and the ridges to the north. Vault toilets and hand pumps for water are in the middle of the loop.

Day-use Facilities: Rollways has a scenic day-use area featuring tables, pedestal grills, and a classic log picnic shelter with fieldstone fireplaces at each end. Many of the tables are within view of the AuSable River and Loud Dam Pond to the east. Nearby a staircase leads down to the river, care should be used when descending. The picnic grounds are open from 6 a.m. to 10 p.m.

Fishing: Rollways is located where the AuSable River flows into Loud Dam Pond. This is no Holy Waters. Upstream from the campground the river is 50 to 75 yards wide and so deep you can't wade it in most places. But anglers say this is where the river yields some of its biggest brown and rainbow trout. Loud Dam Pond is known primarily for smallmouth bass but also yields walleye, perch and northern pike.

Canoeing: Across the road from the campground is *Rollways Resort* (517-728-3322) which runs a canoe livery during the summer. Most paddlers are taken up river to either Alcona County Park, a 23-mile, five-hour trip, or Stewart Creek, a 13-mile, two-hour paddle from the campground.

Season: Rollways' managed season is from the end of May through mid-September. This is a lightly used facility and a site is easy to obtain here even on most weekends.

36

HORSESHOE LAKE
HURON NATIONAL FOREST

Region: Lake Huron
Nearest Community: Glennie
Sites: 9 **Reservations:** No
Fee: $4
Information: Harrisville Ranger (517) 724-5431

The brown national forest sign on M-65 simply says "Campground." It's doesn't say if it is modern or rustic, if it's on a lake or how many sites there are. Go ahead, take a chance and follow the sign.

The best things in life are always unexpected and Horseshoe Lake Campground, located in the heart of the Huron National Forest, turned out to be a real gem the first time my family stayed there. It's a small facility with only nine sites, located on a wooded bluff above a undeveloped lake. And it's a lightly used facility. Though we arrived in mid-July, the height of Michigan's camping season, only one other party occupied a site.

Directions: Horseshoe Lake is 3.5 miles north of Glennie on M-65. From Harrisville head west on M-72 for 22 miles and then south on M-

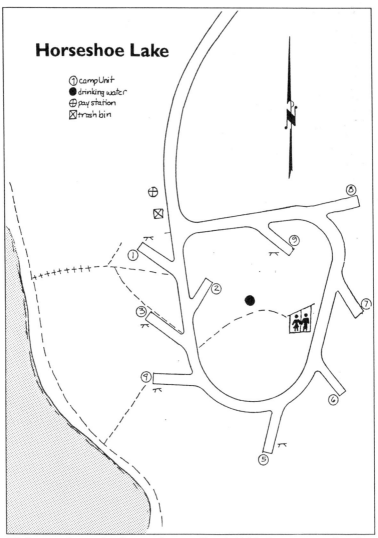

Horseshoe Lake

① camp Unit
● drinking water
⊕ pay station
☒ trash bin

65 for a mile to the Forest Service Road 4124 that is posted with a "Campground" sign. Head a mile west on the dirt road to the entrance.

Campground: Horseshoe Lake is a single loop of nine sites with gravel spurs, tables, and fire rings with sliding grills. The campground is partly shaded and several sites are in a semi-open grassy area but the loop is enclosed by the hilly and heavily forested terrain. Three sites (1, 3 and

4) are on the edge of the bluff with a view of the lake and a direct path down to the water. Other facilities include vault toilets and a hand pump for water.

Fishing: Within the campground is an unimproved launch that's strictly for carry-in boats. But you really don't need anything more for the 16-acre lake that is indeed shaped like a horseshoe. The west half of the lake is the best for fishing and quit deep in the middle. At one time Horseshoe was stocked with rainbow trout but that program has been discontinued. I've always found it a fun lake to catch bass, even though few are of legal size.

Hiking: Near the fee pipe is a marked trailhead for a 1.3-mile loop that winds around the lakeshore to a bench on the opposite shore and then circles back through the rolling hills.

Season: Horseshoe Lake's managed season is mid-April to the end of November. This is a lightly used facility but of course it doesn't take many campers to fill it up. Other nearby campgrounds if it's full are Jewel Lake and Rollways (see page 94).

37

JEWEL LAKE
HURON NATIONAL FOREST

Region: Lake Huron
Nearest Community: Barton City
Sites: 32   **Reservations:** No
Fee: $5
Information: Harrisville Ranger (517) 724-5431

One of the largest campgrounds in the Huron National Forest is Jewel Lake, offering not only numerous sites but several other attractive features. There's a pleasant beach and swimming area, a mile-long nature trail ideal for children, a separate picnic area and fishing opportunities in the large lake.

Very little of Jewel Lake is on National Forest land so expect a shoreline ringed by cottages and heavy traffic for boaters and anglers. Otherwise this is a delightful place for a weekend camping trip.

Directions: From US-23 in Harrisville, head west on M-72 for 14.5

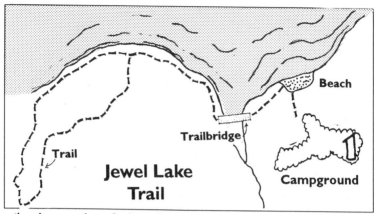

Jewel Lake Trail

Trail

Trailbridge

Beach

Campground

miles then north on Sanborn Road for 1.7 miles and left on Trask Road for 0.7 miles. Jewel Lake has a posted entrance on Trask Road.

Campground: Jewel Lake has 32 gravelled-spur sites with numbers 1-15 on Aspen Loop and 16-32 on Pine Loop. Both loops are lightly shaded and although there are no sites directly on the lake, most of Aspen Loop is only a short walk from the beach and swimming area. Facilities include a handful of vault toilets, two hand pumps for water, tables and fire rings with sliding grills.

Day-use Facilities: The campground has a small picnic area next to its boat launch and separated from the campground by a marsh. Next to Aspen Loop is a delightful beach and marked swimming area with shallow water and a sandy bottom. Be aware that the lake once had a problem with swimmer's itch and it may pay off to double check its status with the Forest Service in Harrisville.

Fishing: Jewel Lake has 193 surface acres and is exceptionally clear. Only the southeast corner of its shoreline is part of the National Forest, the rest of it is privately owned. A cement slab boat launch is located in the picnic area with parking for additional cars and trailers. The lake is best known for panfish but anglers also work its waters for largemouth bass and northern pike.

Hiking: Departing from the beach area is a delightful mile-long loop that in its first half crosses a bridge over a beaver dam and then follows the shoreline of Jewel Lake. The second half winds through an enchanting paper birch forest.

Season: Jewel Lake's managed season is Memorial Day through Labor Day and fills only on the holidays and a rare weekend.

38

AVERY LAKE
MACKINAW STATE FOREST

Region: Lake Huron
Nearest Community: Atlanta
Sites: 19   **Reservations:** No
Fee: $6
Information: Atlanta DNR Office (517) 785-4251

There are two state forest campgrounds, one small and one large, on Avery Lake, a beautiful and somewhat secluded body of water south of Atlanta in Montmorency County. The large facility, with 27 sites, is Big Oaks, but the more popular one is Avery Lake.

It's easy to see why. Built in 1976, Avery Lake is the newest of the two units and offers nice views of the water, a few walk-in sites that tent campers will adore and even a small swimming area. Big Oaks is usually less crowded and more quiet but lacks both being near the lakeshore and a decent place for children to splash around on a hot summer afternoon. Less than a mile separates them and either unit is worth searching out.

Directions: From downtown Atlanta, if there is such a thing, take County Road 487 south as it makes several 90-degree curves in every direction. After 5.5 miles, turn west (right) onto a dirt road posted with a "State Forest Campground" sign. It quickly merges into Avery Lake Road and in 3.5 miles will pass first the posted entrance to Avery Lake then Big Oaks.

Campground: This is a very pleasant facility with 19 sites on two loops in a lightly forested area of predominantly oak. None of the sites are directly on the water but a handful on the second loop are on a high bank overlooking the lower half of the lake. Most are in a wooded setting but the campground does lack the seclusion of most state forest campgrounds.

Sites 15-17 are walk-in and overlook the water but are no more than 20 yards from where you park the car. Nearby is a stairway down to a sandy spot on the lakeshore where children often go swimming. All sites have a table and fire ring while nearby are hand pumps for water and vault

Angler lands a smallmouth bass.

toilets.

Fishing: An improved boat launch with a cement ramp and additional parking is located next to the campground. Avery Lake is 320 acres and most of its southern half is state land with cottage development being confined to the north. It was formed when Crooked Creek was dammed by logs in 1898 and the dam was first rebuilt in 1945 by sportsmen and again in 1971.

At the south end of the lake is Avery Springs while its deepest spot is 78 feet. The predominate species caught are perch, bluegill and largemouth bass. An occasional walleye is pulled out along with northern pike and smallmouth bass. Fishing pressure appears moderate on most weekends, light in the middle of the week.

Season: This campground is smaller and more scenic than Big Oaks thus tends to be more crowded. Still it only fills on an occasional weekend or the holidays.

39

ESS LAKE
MACKINAW STATE FOREST

Region: Lake Huron
Nearest Community: Hillman
Sites: 28   **Reservations:** No
Fee: $6
Information: Gaylord DNR Office (616) 732-3541

Almost since the earliest days of automobile travel, a small peninsula jutting out into Ess Lake has been a popular spot for campers to pull up and an official state campground since 1938. This mid-size lake, with it's productive fishing, clear water and fine beach still draws campers today.

The Forest Management Division enlarged the state forest campground in 1968 with a second loop of 13 sites but the campground still fills weekends during the summer and sometimes by Thursday evening at the height of the camping season. Anglers are especially attracted to this lake because of its no-wake regulations during the prime fishing hours in the morning and evening.

Directions: The campground is 16 miles northeast of Atlanta in Montmorency County. From Atlanta head north on M-33 and then east on County Road 624, reached just after passing Jackson Lake State Forest Campground. The entrance to Ess Lake is 9.5 miles east on CR 624.

Campground: Ess has 28 sites divided on two loops situated almost across from each on the lake. The first loop is connected to the beach and

Pumpkinseed sunfish caught on poppers

day-use area by a foot path and features 13 sites well secluded in a forest of mixed pine and hardwoods. Two sites overlook the water.

The second loop is further from the beach but on a point that gives Ess its horseshoe shape. Almost all of these sites are on the water and 19-25 are on a low bluff with a scenic view of the lake. Both loops have tables, fire rings, hand pumps for water, and vault toilets.

Day-use Facilities: Off the first loop is the day-use area with parking for additional vehicles. Ess features a beach and grassy area and a marked swimming area with a sandy bottom and a gentle slope. A few tables and vault toilets are also located here.

Fishing: The 114-acre lake is heavily developed with cottages and boating traffic can be moderate to heavy on the weekends. For this reason a no-wake regulation is imposed on Ess from 7:30 p.m. to 11 a.m. Near the second loop is a improved boat launch with a cement ramp, dock and limited parking for a handful of vehicles and rigs. Ess has no outlet and ranges in depth up to 50 feet in the middle of the west bay. The lake has been planted with walleyes in the past while anglers also target small-mouth and largemouth bass, perch and pike.

Season: From mid-July through late August Ess can be filled on any weekend and often is at least half filled by Thursday afternoon.

40 OSSINEKE

MACKINAW STATE FOREST

Region: The Tip
Nearest Community: Ossineke
Sites: 42 sites   **Reservations:** No
Fee: $6
Information: Gaylord DNR Office (517) 732-3541

The only state forest campground on Lake Huron is a delightful facility that most travelers heading north on US-23 don't even realize is there. The tendency when passing through the hamlet of Ossineke is to overlook the small brown campground sign...and that's too bad.

The rustic campground is separated from the town, off by itself in a place where you can wander undeveloped stretches of beaches for miles, right into Negwegon State Park if so desired. The facility offers a beautiful beach, sandy swimming area, and even a mile-long pathway where it's possible to spot deer in the early morning.

Directions: The campground is posted at the corner of US-23 and Ossineke Road but the sign is easy to miss. Turn east onto Ossineke Road and follow it to another state forest sign at the corner of State Road. Turn right on State Road and drive to the entrance at the end.

Campground: Ossineke has 42 sites on two loops winding along Lake Huron. The first loop has sites 1-26 of which 19 of them, including 18-26, are right off the water. Most have a thin line of trees or brush separating them from the sandy beach but three are out in the open with a clear and beautiful view of the Great Lake. These sites for the most part are in a stand of white and red pine with little undergrowth and thus little privacy.

The second loop (sites 27-42) is situated in an oak/maple forest. The sites are more spread out and secluded from each other but not as close to the stretch of beach favored by swimmers. Fire rings, tables, hand pumps for water and vault toilets are on each loop.

Day-use Facilities: A small picnic area with a handful of tables and pedestal grills is located within the west loop and closes at 10 p.m. The beach here is beautiful, most years a wide sandy strip most with a shallow

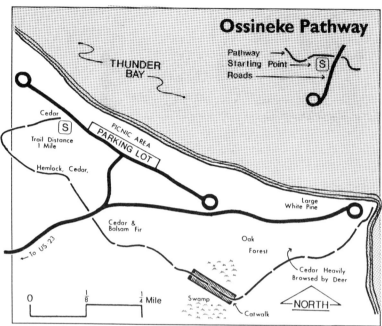

water and a soft bottom ideal for young swimmers even if there is no marked swimming area. On a clear summer day you can enjoy a view from the water towers of Alpena to Scarecrow Island of the Michigan Island National Wildlife Refuge to the south. The campground has no boat launch on the lake.

Hiking: *Ossineke Pathway* is a one-mile trail that begins next to site 14 and ends near site 42 of the second loop. You start off in an upland forest of a wide variety of trees ranging from white and red pine to oak, beech, paper birch and maple. The trail winds across the entrance drive and then swings through a low lying forest, passing several grassy meadows and even crossing a boardwalk through a swamp.

You can also hike the beach south along one of the most undeveloped stretches of Lake Huron and within six miles reach South Point in Negwegon State Park. The shoreline switches from beautiful sandy bays and beaches to rocky shorelines. Two miles beyond South Point is the state park's parking area and water pump.

Season: Ossineke experiences moderate use on weekends in mid-July through mid-August but getting a site anytime during the summer is usually easy.

41

JACKSON LAKE
MACKINAW STATE FOREST

Region: The Tip
Nearest Community: Atlanta
Sites: 18   **Reservations:** No
Fee: $6
Information: Atlanta DNR Office (517) 785-4251

Built in 1963, Jackson Lake is a small, rustic campground often overlooked by travelers heading north from Atlanta on their way to Clear Lake State Park. The two state facilities are connected together by the Clear Lake-Jackson Lake Trail but the similarities end there.

The state park has 200 sites, the state forest campground a mere 18 sites. Jackson Lake is not nearly as large or deep as the 133-acre Clear Lake, nor does it attracts as much motor boat activity. There are a few cottages on Jackson Lake but not so many as to prevent a pair of loons from nesting here annually and for state biologists to post a Loon Alert within the campground.

Directions: From Atlanta, head north on M-33 and you soon pass the DNR Field Office (open Monday through Friday 8 a.m. to 5 p.m.) where maps of area trails can be picked up. Jackson Lake is six miles north of Atlanta and posted along M-33.

Campground: Jackson Lake has a loop of 18 sites with seven of them overlooking the shoreline. The area is forested in pines and hardwoods with moderate undergrowth and the sites are well separated. Facilities include tables and grills, though some sites are lacking either, vault toilets, and hand pumps for water within the loop.

Day-Use Facilities: Jackson Lake has a small picnic area with a few tables and pedestal grills located on a scenic point jutting out from the campground. It's a nice place to enjoy lunch as you can view the entire lake from your table.

Fishing: There is no improved ramp for trailers but launching a hand-carried boat is no problem. Jackson Lake has 25 surface acres and is 26 feet at its deepest point with no inlet of any kind. Some anglers target

Lady Slipper Orchids found near the Clear Lake-Jackson Lake Trail.

largemouth bass and northern pike but the lake is best fished for perch bluegill and other species of panfish.

Hiking: Located within the campground is the southern trailhead for the *Clear Lake-Jackson Lake Trail,* a loop between the two campgrounds on both sides of M-33. In the winter it's a nice backcountry ski but it passes too many cottages, roads and clearcuts to be an enjoyable hike. The entire loop makes for a 7.5-mile trek and along the way you pass an intersection with the *High County Pathway.*

Season: This is a lightly used campground where often in the middle of the week there is only one or two parties if any at all. Sites should be easy to obtain even on the weekends.

42

TUBBS ISLAND
PERE MARQUETTE STATE FOREST

Region: Heartland
Nearest Community: Barryton
Sites: 12   **Reservations:** No
Fee: $6
Information: Mecosta County Parks (616) 832-3246

There are two state forest campgrounds on Tubbs Lake in Mecosta County. The first is located on the east shore and is called, simply enough, Tubbs Lake Campground. It has 21 sites, many of them right on the water, and all of them secluded in a well forested area that is typical of most state forest facilities.

It's a nice place to spend a weekend but the second campground is nicer. It's an island.

What originally was a hill overlooking the west side of the lake is now Tubbs Island when the surrounded areas were flooded to create a waterfowl habitat known as Martiny Flooding. But you don't need a boat to reach it.

Tubbs Island is reached by driving across a narrow dike and once on the island you'll discover a delightful state forest campground where there is a view of water or marshes from every site. The state forest facility is managed by Mecosta County Park Commission, no doubt the reason it's so well maintained. While there are only 12 sites, two are walk-in and often are available for tent campers when the rest of the loop is filled.

The only drawback is the lack swimming in the campground and the large number of cottages along the south shore of Tubbs Lake.

Directions: From US-10, head south on M-66, pass through the town of Barryton and in 12 miles turn west on 17 Mile Road for 1.5 miles. Turn south of 45th Avenue and then west on Madison Road and in a little over a mile you'll pass the posted entrance to Tubbs Lake State Forest Campground. The posted drive to Tubbs Island State Forest Campground is another two miles west.

Young angler with a his first bluegill from Tubbs Lake.

Campground: It's easy to understand the popularity of Tubbs Island; every site overlooks the water. There is a single loop of 10 drive-in sites, located in a lightly forested area of hardwoods with views of either Tubbs Lake or marshy Lost Lake to the west. The last two sites are designated as walk-in and are located at the top of the island in a semi-open area that has a great view of the lakes as well as all your neighbors below. Campers park their vehicles along the loop and walk 30 yards to where they can pitch their tent. All sites have tables and fire rings while vault toilets and hand pumps for water are along the loop.

Fishing: The 116-acre lake is an excellent fishery that includes northern pike, perch, largemouth bass, and black crappies. But it's best known as a panfish lake with bluegills and pumpkinseed sunfish. Tubbs Lake isn't stocked and hasn't been since 1941.

There is a fish cleaning station and an improved boat ramp on the island along with parking for a few vehicles and trailers. But bluegills and sunfish can also be caught from shore with simple bobber rigs, making the lake an ideal fishery for children. In all, there are six public boat ramps accessing the Martiny Flooding which is composed of six lakes, though many are little more than a small opening in a cattail marsh.

Season: The campground is generally open from early April through mid-November, closing when it too hazardous to drive across the dike. It will often be filled weekends from late June through August.

WAGNER LAKE
HURON NATIONAL FOREST

Region: Heartland
Nearest Community: Mio
Sites: 12   **Reservations:** No
Fee: $5
Information: Mio Ranger (517) 826-3717

Wagner Lake is a small body of water 7 miles south of Mio and completely surrounded by National Forest land. Bordering its east side is a small campground. One compliments the other extremely well and a stay here is usually a quiet, relaxing night on the shore of a scenic lake.

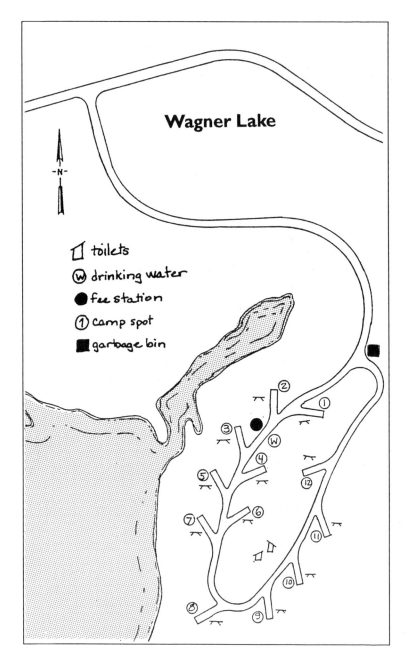

Wagner Lake

-N-

- ⌂ toilets
- Ⓦ drinking water
- ● fee station
- ① camp spot
- ◼ garbage bin

The key is getting a site.

With only 12 sites, Wagner Lake tends to be full most weekends from late June through mid-August. The facility is rustic but its paved interior road and spurs make it especially popular with RV campers. Site availability is on a first-come-first-serve basis and to ensure getting a spot, plan on arriving Wednesday evening or Thursday morning.

No official hiking trails are nearby and the beach is limited but there is good bluegill fishing in a lake small enough to be easily handled in a canoe or cartop rowboat.

Directions: From Rose City head north on M-33 for 9 miles then turn west (left) on Wagner Lake Road, a dirt road that passes the paved entrance of the campground in 1.2 miles. Wagner Lake Road is 7 miles south from M-72 and M-33 in Mio.

Campground: The campground is a single loop of 12 paved sites in an area wooded in both pines and towering hardwoods. Both the loop and sites can be easily handled by the largest motor homes while in the middle of the loop is a pair of vault toilets and a hand pump for water. Half of the sites are just up from the shoreline with a full view of the lake. The other half is located on a gently sloping hillside and still provide partial views of the water.

Day-use Facilities: The campground features a small sandy beach with a marked swimming area that is shallow. Though there is a visitor's parking lot near it, the beach is limited to campers only.

Fishing: Wagner Lake has 26 surface areas and is free from cottages or docks to provide a pleasant angling experience in a scenic setting. The fishing must be good at times as a few locals often stash a small boat along the shore here and there. Forest Service rangers report fisheries of bluegill, bass and perch but without a doubt this is primarily panfish waters. Bluegill fishing is good while most bass landed tend to measure less than 10 inches in length.

There is no boat launch within the campground, making hand-carried boats ideal here. Children and other boatless anglers can follow a sandy path along the north side of the lake and have few problems reaching any stretch of the shore.

Season: The managed season is from Memorial Day through Labor Day but if spring weather is warm the park hosts begin collecting fees earlier. This campground is often filled on the weekend in July and August.

ISLAND LAKE
HURON NATIONAL FOREST

Region: Heartland
Nearest Community: Rose City
Sites: 17   **Reservations:** No
Fee: $5 to $6
Information: Mio Ranger (517) 826-3252

First impressions can be misleading. Take Island Lake Campground for example. The first thing many people notice driving through the Huron National Forest campground are the cottages bordering the loop.

And then maybe the cottages across from the small beach, cottages all along the shoreline of the 65-acre lake, cottages everywhere.

Ugh! How do you escape?

You pitch your tent in one of the lightly shaded sites that overlook the water, throw swim suits and towels in a small pack and lose yourself along the Island Lake Nature Trail on your way to Loon Lake Recreation Area. Within minutes you're trudging up a ridge, deep in a woods of impressive oaks and an occasional towering white pine and seemingly miles from anywhere, not a cottage insight.

The campground and nearby day-use area are linked together by foot trails and together make for an excellent place to camp, providing opportunities for limited hiking, fishing, boating or just wiggling your toes in two different beaches.

Directions: From I-75 depart onto M-33 (exit 202) and head north through Rose City. Six miles north of the town turn west on County Road 486 to first pass the entrance of Loon Lake. The campground is another half mile along CR 486.

Campground: The campground is a single loop located on a gently sloping hillside leading down to Island Lake. The 17 sites feature paved parking spurs, fire rings with sliding grills and tables while nearby are four vault toilets and two hand pumps for water. The sites are lightly shaded with little privacy between them and cottages border each side of the campground. But one rents out canoes, rowboats and pedalboats to

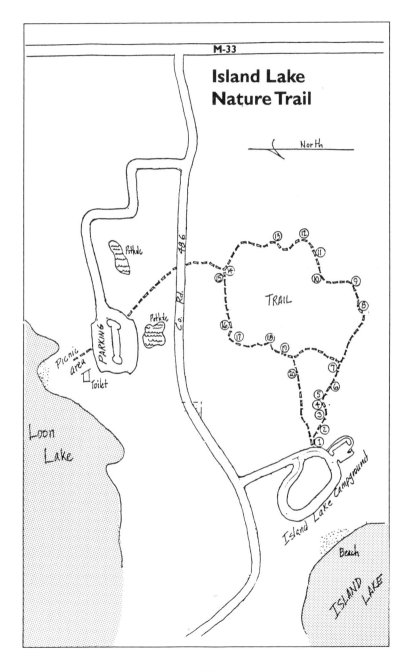

**Island Lake
Nature Trail**

campers and the other sells firewood.

Day-use Facilities: There is a small day-use area within Island Lake composed of a parking area, grassy area with tables and pedestal grills and a thin strip of beach overlooking a marked swimming area. Hours are 6 a.m. to 10 p.m.

But Loon Lake Recreation Area is far better and worth the two-minute drive or the 0.8-mile hike. The 90-acre lake has few visible cottages on it, most of the north and west shore is national forest and the beach is wider than at Island Lake. There is also a bathhouse with flush toilets, tables, pedestal grills, and drinking fountains. There is no fee to enter Loon Lake in a vehicle.

Hiking: The trail is basically a one-mile loop with a spur near post number 14 leading off to Loon Lake, crossing County Road 486 along the way. It is a 1.4-mile round trip to the lake through an area laden with glacial evidence in the form of morainal hills and potholes. Along the way you pass 20 numbered posts that correspond to a pamphlet available from the campground manager. Posts pointed out everything from where a lightning bolt struck a red pine to an 1890 logging trail.

Fishing: There are no boat ramps at either facility although hand-carried boats could be easily launched. Island Lake is 65 acres large with fair fishing for perch, rock bass, bluegill and largemouth bass, though it's rare to see any bass larger than 12 inches here. There is a ban on boat motors in the lake.

Loon lake is larger, more clear and generally considered to have a better fishery, particularly for largemouth bass but also yellow perch and bluegill. Although there is no public boat ramp here, *Loon Lake Campground* (517-685-2407) off of M-33 has bait and boats for rent.

Season: Island Lake is managed by a campground host from Memorial Day through Labor Day. It will often be filled during the weekends but obtaining a site in mid-week is not too difficult.

 **NEWAYGO**
STATE PARK

Region: Heartland
Nearest Community: Oxbow
Sites: 99   **Reservations:** Yes
Fee: $6
Information: Park contact station (616) 856-4452

Newaygo is one of the few units of the state park system with a rustic campground and where there is actually a little space and privacy between sites. For these reasons the 257-acre park is also one of the few rustic facilities that can easily be filled on almost any weekend in the summer.

Located on the shores of Hardy Dam Pond southwest of Big Rapids, the park features little beyond its campground and a boat launch. But the fishing is moderately good in the man-made lake and the campground is a splendid place to park a trailer in October when the facility is empty and the surrounding hardwoods are at the peak of autumn blaze of color.

Directions: The park is 43 miles north of Grand Rapids and can be reached from US-131. Depart west on Jefferson Road at the Morley exit for 7 miles and then head north on Beech Road to the park's entrance.

Campground: Newaygo has 99 sites spread out on two loops. *Oak Campground* features sites 1-48 in a forest of young hardwoods and moderate undergrowth, providing privacy that is usually not associated with state parks. No sites are on the water but a path from the back of the loop leads to a bluff where you view most of the reservoir. Depending on the water level, a small beach lies below the bluff here.

Sites 49-99 are located in *Poplar Campground* where campers set up in a forest of slightly older hardwoods. A couple of sites are a few feet from the edge of the bluff overlooking the lake but the rest, like Oak Campground, are tucked into the trees and out of sight of the water. Both loops have limited playground equipment, vault toilets, hand pumps for water, tables, and fire rings.

Fishing: Newaygo features an improved boat launch along with a dock and parking for 50 additional vehicles and trailers on a small inlet of Hardy Dam Pond. The lake, with the "the third largest earthen-filled dam

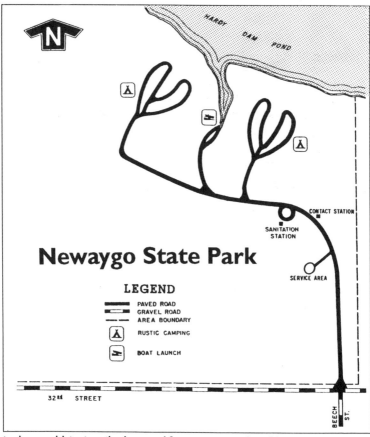

in the world, is six miles long and features more than 50 miles of shoreline that is dotted with campgrounds and boat ramps. It's stocked annually with walleyes and also was one of a handful of lakes where an experimental early bass season was held. Anglers were allowed to catch and release bass beginning April 1 and then keep legal ones after the statewide season opened on the Saturday preceding Memorial Day.

Season: Newaygo is open from May through October and, despite being a rustic facility, often fills up on weekends from mid-July to early August. During the week it's easy to obtain a site as well as before July 4 and after mid-August. During the summer the contact station is staffed and can book site reservations. If it is closed, call Silver Lake State Park at (616) 873-3083.

46

HEMLOCK
MANISTEE NATIONAL FOREST

Region: Heartland
Nearest Community: Cadillac
Sites: 15   **Reservations:** No
Fee: $5 to $8
Information: Cadillac Ranger (616) 775-8539

A rustic and much more quiet alternative to the William Mitchell State Park is Hemlock on a back bay of Lake Mitchell just five miles east of Cadillac. Unlike the large and compact campground at the state park that borders M-119, an extremely busy road during the summer, Hemlock is a considerably smaller facility with a wooded appearance while still providing access to fisheries of Lake Mitchell and Lake Cadillac.

The drawback is the national forest campground does not have a swimming area of any kind and it tends to fill up as often as the state park, where at least you can book a site in advance.

Directions: From US-131, head north on M-115 and then just before reaching Mitchell State Park, turn west on M-55. Within a mile turn right on Pole Road and the campground entrance is reached in another mile.

Campground: Hemlock is a managed campground of 15 rustic sites. The loop is paved and so are the spurs with many of them pull-throughs ideal for large RVs. The sites are well separated and secluded in an area that includes both a pine plantation and stand of spruce and hardwoods.

Six sites are labeled lakefront and cost more but only a few of them actually overlook the water and provide direct access to the lake. The others, most notably site 14, overlook the heavy growth of cattails along the shore not the water. Lakefront sites (5, 7, 9, 11, 13, and 14) are $8 per night. Off-lake sites (1-4, 6, 10, 12, and 15) are $5 per night.

Day-use Facilities: Near the boat launch are a few tables and fire rings including two on each side of the ramp that overlook the entire back bay. Otherwise there is no swimming area nor any hiking trails.

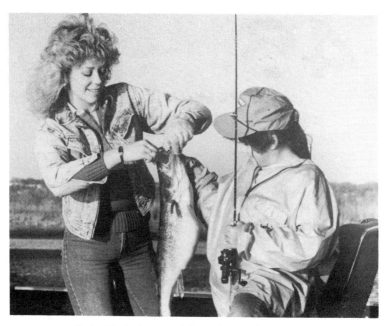

Lake Mitchell is noted for its fine walleye fishery

Fishing: An improved ramp with a metal grate bottom is situated on the lake along with parking for a handful of vehicles. The back bay is for the most part undeveloped except for cottages and docks near its entrance. Most of the shore supports a heavy growth of cattails, reeds and other aquatic plant life, the reason, no doubt you always see a good number of anglers.

Both Mitchell and Cadillac are known as fine walleye fisheries and are heavily fished during the summer. The 1,150-acre Lake Cadillac is an extremely busy body of water as it lies totally within the city limits of Cadillac and its shoreline is totally developed. For that reason many anglers prefer the 2,580-acre Mitchell which also supports walleyes as well as perch, various panfish and bass. You can put in at Hemlock and reach Cadillac by a quarter-mile canal that runs along the state park and connects the two lakes.

Season: Hemlock is open year-round but provides services from only Memorial Day to Labor Day. Because of its close proximity to Cadillac, the facility fills up most weekends July through August and often during the middle of the week.

47

GOOSE LAKE
PERE MARQUETTE STATE FOREST

Region: Heartland
Nearest Community: Lake City
Sites: 54   **Reservations:** No
Fee: $6
Information: Cadillac DNR office (616) 775-9727

Goose Lake is the largest state forest campground in the Lower Peninsula and when combined with Long Lake provides almost 70 sites on the neighboring lakes. That is a lot of campsites, yet on many summer weekends these facilities are nearly filled.

Located just northwest of Lake City in a hilly and scenic section of the Pere Marquette State Forest, Goose Lake offers everything most campers seek in a rustic facility. There is good swimming and fishing opportunities and a choice of sites with many overlooking the sandy shoreline of this horseshoe-shaped lake. If this facility has too many campers for you, then just continue along the forest road to Long Lake (page 120), a much smaller and more remote campground.

Directions: From Lake City head north on M-66 and then west (left) on Sanborn Road to Al Moses Road. Here state forest signs direct you west along Goose Lake Road, a well-graded dirt road that leads to the entrance of Goose Lake within a mile. You have to drive through the campground and continue on the forest road to reach Long Lake.

Campground: Strung out along the northern shore, Goose Lake has 54 sites with most of them gathered in a half dozen small loops. Many sites are located right on the water or within view of the lake and a few are even situated on a high shoreline bank, an especially scenic spot from your tent.

Most of the sites along the lake are close together and lack privacy but those on the other side of the road, away from the water, are well separated and secluded in a young hardwood forest. Vault toilets and hand pumps for water are scattered throughout the campground but many tables and fire rings are missing.

Day-Use Facility: There isn't a day-use beach or marked swimming area but much of the lake's shoreline is sandy and shallow, making it pleasant for swimming.

Fishing: An improved boat ramp with a cement slab is located within the campground but small boats can be launched from many shoreline sites. Goose Lake is a horseshoe-shaped body of water with a point in the middle and an island on its west side. Its eastern arm is narrow and very weedy but the west arm is free of heavy aquatic growth in the middle and holds the deepest sections. Panfish are plentiful though a bluegill over 10 inches seems to be a rare catch. Anglers also target smallmouth bass and occasionally catch small northern pike.

Season: Goose Lake is managed by a campground host and on July and August weekends can be more than three-quarters filled by Saturday afternoon. The first sites to go, naturally, are those along the lake's sandy shoreline.

48

LONG LAKE
PERE MARQUETTE STATE FOREST

Region: Heartland
Nearest Community: Lake City
Sites: 16   **Reservations:** No
Fee: $6
Information: Cadillac DNR Office (616) 775-9727

Long Lake is reached by first driving through Goose Lake campground and then following a one-way loop past several ponds before arriving at the small lake. On the way back you skirt a bluff with an overlook of Goose Lake, all part of this very hilly and scenic area just northwest of Lake City.

If you want a large campground with lakeview sites and lots of sandy shoreline for swimming, stop at Goose Lake. If you want a small, somewhat remote and quieter facility on a lake of its own, continue on to Long Lake. Many people do, the reason Long Lake is occasionally full on a summer weekend while Goose Lake has open sites.

Directions: From Lake City head north on M-66 and then west (left)

Long Lake in Pere Marquette State Forest near Lake City.

on Sanborn Road to Al Moses Road. Here state forest signs direct you west along Goose Lake Road that in a mile arrives at the entrance of Goose Lake State Forest Campground. You have to drive through the campground and continue on the forest road to reach Long Lake.

Campground: Located on the northeast corner of the lake are 16 sites. Half of them are right on the shoreline with a scenic view of the length of this long and narrow body of water. The forest here is hardwoods with little undergrowth and sites tend to be close together.

There is no marked swimming area or beach, but the edges of Long Lake are sandy and shallow, making it possible for children to enjoy some swimming activity.

Fishing: There is an unimproved boat launch near the end of the campground. The middle of Long Lake is free of heavy aquatic plants but lily pads are thick at the north end. The lake supports smallmouth bass, bluegill and some pike. Overall there is less fishing pressure here than Goose Lake because of the size of the campground. Most anglers arrive with canoes or small rowboats and the lake is so narrow it could even be tackled in a belly boat.

Season: Long Lake usually has its own campground host and because of its limited number of sites will occasionally fill up on a July or early August weekend.

49

LEVERENTZ LAKES
PERE MARQUETTE STATE FOREST

Region: Heartland
Nearest Community: Baldwin
Sites: 17   **Reservations:** No
Fee: $6
Information: Baldwin DNR office (616) 745-4651

Is this one or two campgrounds? There are two separate loops, each with own entrance, each on their own lake, each with own vault toilets and other facilities. Yet the numbering system that begins on the sites along Big Leverentz Lake finish on Little Leverentz Lake.

Does it matter? Either way this is a delightful place to camp with lake-view sites, good fishing opportunities and a trail system that wanders into the woods. Best of all, despite its close proximity to Baldwin, it does not receive an overload of campers and other users.

Directions: The campground is northeast of Baldwin and can be reached by heading east on US-10 for 2 miles and then north on Mud Trail. Immediately turn west (left) on Campground Road and follow signs to either lake. The campgrounds are posted along both US-10 and on Campground Road.

Campground: Big Leverentz has 10 sites on two loops along the south side of the lake. Eight sites are situated on one loop with most of them on a low rise for a nice view of the water. The other two are off by themselves near the boat launch and all of them are well spread out in a mixed stand of pines and hardwoods with moderate undergrowth.

Little Leverentz is to the south and has seven sites on a single loop. The area is a little more forested in pine but only one site is on the water while within view are the backsides of several cottages. Both feature vault toilets, hand pumps for water, fire rings and tables.

Fishing: On Big Leverentz there is an unimproved dirt boat launch and additional parking for two maybe three vehicles within the campground. Next to the launch is a very nice T-shaped dock and, in a lake this small, you can reach a lot of water with a good cast from here. The lake

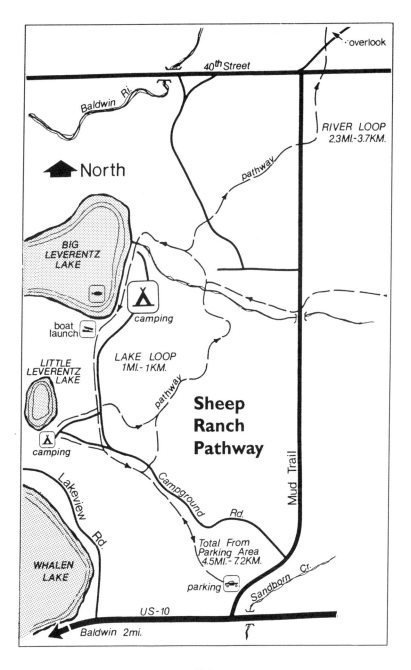

is completely undeveloped an _ its west side is heavy weeded with aquatic plants and lily pads but the rest is clear. For the most part Big Leverentz is panfish waters with an occasional bluegill reaching nine to 10 inches but most of them small. Every once in a while somebody will also pull out a largemouth bass.

There is no launch on Little Leverentz but a pathway next to site number 14 leads to the shoreline. The lake is the better of the two though it is slightly smaller at 5.6 acres. It has a weedy shoreline but the middle is 30 feet deep. Little Leverentz contains bluegill, pumpkinseed and perch along with largemouth bass and northern pike and attracts moderate pressure in the summer and even less in the winter.

Hiking: The trailhead for *Sheep Ranch Pathway* is posted in Big Leverentz. It's composed of several loops including the River Loop, a 2.3 mile trek to an overlook on the Baldwin River to the north. Because of clearcuts and cars and other trash dumped in the woods, this pathway is a far better ski trail in the winter than it is for hikers during the summer.

Season: Big Leverentz is the more popular of the two lakes and will occasionally fill up on a July or August weekend but not often due to the large number of state and national campgrounds in the Baldwin area.

SILVER CREEK
PERE MARQUETTE STATE FOREST

Region: Heartland
Nearest Community: Luther
Sites: 25 sites   **Reservations:** No
Fee: $6
Information: Baldwin DNR office (616) 745-4651

No matter how you arrive at Silver Creek State Forest Campground, whether it's in the bow of a canoe or the backseat of a car, this is a delightful spot to spend a night or even a few days.

The Pine River is one of the state's blue ribbon trout streams as well as one of the most popular canoe routes during the summer. You can paddle downstream, hike along its banks upstream or just sit in your

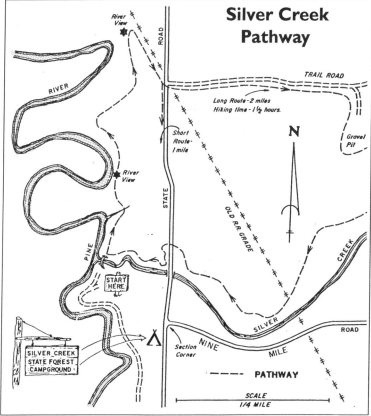

riverbend campsite dabbling a worm in hopes of landing a trout.

The rustic facility features many sites along the water along with a handful of walk-in sites and is not nearly as busy as the national forest campgrounds downstream. The only drawback for some people is the off-road vehicle trail that passes nearby. But most ORV riders, and thus their activity, tend to congregate at Lincoln Bridge State Forest Campground located a mile to the north along State Road.

Directions: Silver Creek is located north of Baldwin and west of Cadillac. From US-131 the campground is reached by exiting onto Luther Highway and heading west for Luther, a small town on the banks of the Little Manistee River. At Luther head north on State Road for 6 miles to the posted entrance of the facility.

Campground: Situated along a single loop are 19 sites in a forest of young beech and other hardwoods with a thick undergrowth. The sites are well spread out and secluded from each other while a handful are right on the river, some so close people set up lawn chairs in front of their trailer and fish for trout. All sites feature the usual fire rings, tables, hand pumps, and vault toilets.

Another six sites are walk-in or canoe sites located on a point formed by a big horseshoe curve in the Pine River. Most overlook this gentle river and no. 23 is one of the best riverbank sites in the Lower Peninsula as it's shaded by several tall cedar and spruce trees and lies above a small stretch of rapids. The parking lot is less than 25 yards from the walk-in sites.

Fishing: The Pine is regarded as a good to excellent trout stream with brook and rainbow trout last planted in the early 1970s. This far up the river the Pine is 10-15 yards wide and wadable in most places while fishing pressure is moderate. Most anglers toss worms or small spinners into deep pools, under log jams and pass undercut banks for primarily brown trout. Brook trout tend to dominate the river upstream near Skookum Bridge. Use the Silver Creek Pathway to gain access to the river down stream.

Hiking: The *Silver Creek Pathway* begins near site no. 10 and quickly crosses the creek near its confluence with the Pine, a popular swimming spot for children staying in the campground. Once on the other side the pathway can either be an easy 1.5-mile trek or a 2.5-mile hike of moderate difficulty if continued along the east side of State Road. The most scenic stretch by far is the first mile which parallels the river much of the way, providing an excellent view of the Pine from a bluff above. The longer loop is poorly marked in some sections.

Canoeing: The Pine flows 60 miles from near Leroy until it merges into the Manistee River near Stronach Dam in Manistee County. To paddle the river in national forest land, you need a free permit between May and October and they can be reserved in advance by calling the Permit Station on M-55 at (616) 862-3333. The first put-in is Edgett's Bridge on Raymond Road and from here it's a five-hour paddle to Silver Creek. The last take-out point is Low Bridge on M-55, a nine-hour paddle for most people. Canoes and transportation can be arranged at *Jarolim Canoes* (616-862-3475), *Baldwin Canoes* (616-745-4669) or *Carl's Canoe Livery* (616-797-5156).

Season: The only time this campground is filled on the weekends is when a large group of canoeists pass through but that is rare this far upstream.

51

KNEFF LAKE
HURON NATIONAL FOREST

Region: Northwest
Nearest Community: Grayling
Sites: 26   **Reservations:** No
Fee: $5
Information: Mio Ranger (517) 826-3717

In an area of Michigan blessed with numerous campgrounds, Kneff Lake is a delightful little facility that is worth searching for. Although the national forest campground could be filled on a mid-summer weekend it doesn't seem to draw the heavy pressure that Hartwick Pines State Park to the north does or some of the state forest facilities west of Grayling along M-72.

Yet Kneff Lake features an excellent beach and picnic area and a hilly terrain that allows sites to be well separated and secluded from each other. Kneff is also a designated trout lake but many anglers are dismayed when they arrive to discover that it lacks a boat ramp or any other kind of launch facility.

Directions: From the Business Loop I-75 in the heart of Grayling head east on M-72 for 6.5 miles and then south (right) on Stephan Bridge Road. In 1.4 miles turn east (left) on Forest Road 4003 and the entrance of the campground is reached in a half mile.

Campground: Sites 1-18 are located on Jack Pine Loop and 19-26 on Oak Loop with both on a high bluff that surrounds the lake. Sites 9 and 12 actually have a partial view of the water but the rest are in a forest of predominantly oak with moderate undergrowth and while you can't see the lake you can't see your neighbor either. A posted trail from each loop leads down to the beach and all sites have a table, fire ring with sliding grill, lantern post, and gravelled parking spurs. The campground also has vault toilets and spigots for water.

Day-use Facilities: Kneff Lake has a picnic area separate from the campground loops with tables and pedestal grills that are well spread out. But the best part is the beach. The sand here is 15 to 20 yards wide and

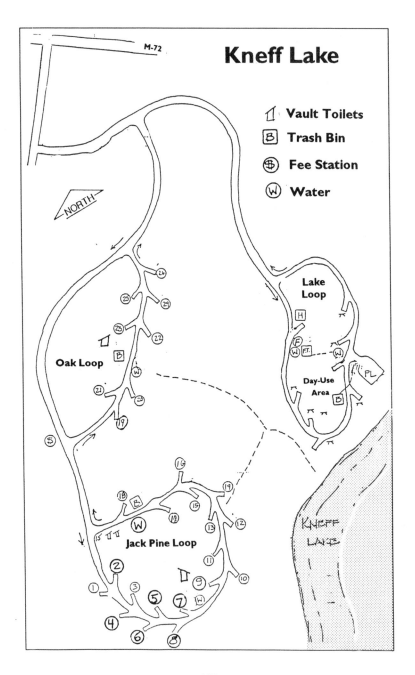

Kneff Lake

M-72

⚓ **Vault Toilets**

Ⓑ **Trash Bin**

⑂ **Fee Station**

Ⓦ **Water**

NORTH

Lake Loop

Oak Loop

Day-Use Area

Jack Pine Loop

KNEFF LAKE

enclosed by extensive log terraces. A swimming area is marked off but beware; the water is cold and the bottom slopes off quickly.

Fishing: The 14-acre lake lies mostly in national forest land with the exception of a few cottages on the south end. It's a cold and deep lake, with depths of 40 to 50 feet, and once was stocked with grayling in a failed attempt to bring the fish back in the late 1980s. Today it's stocked with rainbow trout with most anglers using slip bobbers to fish worms right off the bottom of the lake. There is no boat launch but it's easy to carry a canoe down to the water through the picnic area. A belly boat would be perfect here.

Hiking: A network of foot trails spans from site to site, down to the beach and through the surrounding hills. Most of them are the result of heavy ORV abuse in the past. Now the area is slowly repairing itself while "Foot Travel Welcome" signs have been posted around the campground.

Season: Kneff has a campground host and is managed from Memorial Day through Labor Day. Occasionally the facility will be full on a weekend but usually you can count on getting a site.

52

KEYSTONE LANDING
AU SABLE STATE FOREST

Region: Northwest
Nearest Community: Grayling
Sites: 18   **Reservations:** No
Fee: $6
Information: Grayling DNR Office (517) 373-1220

A fly fisher's haven, Keystone Landing is one of a handful of state forest facilities along the Au Sable River. It is a scenic facility overlooking the legendary Holy Waters stretch of the Au Sable and used by both anglers and canoeists. But the campground is not big and with only 18 sites it's easy for Keystone Landing to fill up. Fortunately the Grayling area is the land of plenty as far as state forest campgrounds are concerned.

Directions: From the junction of Business Loop I-75 in Grayling, head east on M-72 and then in 6 miles turn north (left) on Keystone

Fly fishers choose a fly on the Au Sable.

Landing Road where the campground is posted.

Campground: Keystone Landing is a single loop of 18 sites located on a high bluff along the south bank of the Au Sable. The area is heavily forested with the sites well spread out and secluded from each other. Yet you can wander to the edge of the bluff and spend a quiet evening watching the rings of rising trout and the fly fishermen they entice. Tables, fire rings, hand pump for water and vault toilets are provided.

Fishing: This stretch of the Au Sable is part of the Holy Waters, a flies-only, no-kill quality fishing area with a year-round season. The river is 30-yards wide here, ranging from two to four feet in depth and for the most part can be waded. In May and June this is one of the most popular sections of the Au Sable for fly fishermen to catch both brown and brook trout.

A pair of stairs in the campground provide easy access down to the river for wader-attired anglers. You can also drive past the entrance of the campground and park at the end of Keystone Landing Road where there is a public access site.

Canoeing: The Au Sable is almost as famous a canoe route as it is a trout stream. As few paddlers put in above Grayling, the river makes for a 135-mile journey to Oscoda on Lake Huron. The most popular stretch is from Grayling to Mio, after that a handful of dams and much wide water are encountered.

There are seven state forest campgrounds posted in the river for canoeists between Grayling and Mio, including Keystone Landing. A number of canoe liveries work the Au Sable, including *Ray's Canoes* (517-348-5844) and *Carlisle Canoes* (517-348-2301) in Grayling and *Watters Edge Canoe Livery* (517-275-5568) in Roscommon.

Season: From early May through June this campground can be filled any weekend with fly fishermen. In July and August, it can be canoeists who take up all the sites but you shouldn't have any problem staying here midweek through most of the summer.

LAKE MARGRETHE
AU SABLE STATE FOREST

Region: Northwest
Nearest Community: Grayling
Sites: 40   **Reservations:** No
Fee: $6
Information: Grayling DNR Office (517) 348-6371

This might be the only campground in Michigan with signs along one side that say "Military Boundary". But don't worry about neighboring Camp Grayling or tanks rolling through the sites and missiles streaking overhead.

Lake Margrethe is a large but peaceful facility situated in the hilly terrain along the west shore of this popular lake. There is a variety of sites available, including some secluded walk-ins, others on the lakeshore and even a handicapped-access sites. The only drawback of Lake Margrethe is its popularity, often filled on the weekends, and the lack of a boat launch.

Directions: The campground is five miles west of Grayling. From M-72 turn south onto McIntyre Landing Road.

Campground: Lake Margrethe has 40 sites spread out along many loops on the west side of the lake. The hilly shoreline makes this a beautiful campground with most of it forested in pine and hardwoods. More than half of the sites are situated right on the water with a fine view of this huge lake while others are merely across the park road.

A dozen of the sites, including seven of the first eight, are walk-in; you park your car and haul the tent to the site. Sites 1-3 are at the south end of the campground, off by themselves right on the lake, for a somewhat secluded setting. Sites 35-38 and a few others are up on a small hill from where you park the car and provide a unique overview of the lake.

Overall the sites are close together and lack the privacy of most state forest campgrounds. Number 32 is a handicapped reserved site, located next to a barrier-free vault toilet and near a special wood ramp and deck onto the lake. Facilities include vault toilets, hand pumps for water, fire rings and tables.

Day-use Facilities: A beach and picnic area is located just north of the campground and consists of a separate parking lot and a handful of tables in an open grassy area. No real beach here but the swimming is excellent with shallow water and a sandy bottom in a lake that is gin clear.

Fishing: Unfortunately there is no boat launch within the campground and the nearest public facility is at the south end of the lake in Camp Grayling. Hand carried boats can easily be launched from most sites and larger crafts can be beached there.

The mile-wide Lake Margrethe is 1,920-acres large and well developed. An all-sports lake, there is considerable use by motor boaters, water skiers, jet skiers and others. The lake is a warm-water fishery best known for smallmouth bass and muskies though the bulk of its catch by anglers is probably bluegill and other panfish.

Season: Despite 40 sites, Lake Margrethe's location just off M-72 and the heavy recreational use of its waters makes it a popular facility. Expect it to be filled any weekend from July through August and occasionally in the middle of the week.

54

UPPER MANISTEE RIVER
AU SABLE STATE FOREST

Region: Northwest
Nearest Community: Frederic
Sites: 50   **Reservations:** No
Fee: $6
Information: Grayling DNR Office (517) 373-1220

There are eight state forest campgrounds on the Manistee River and the most visible, and thus the most popular, facility is eight miles west of Grayling where M-72 crosses the famous trout stream. But if you camp to get away and value a little solitude in the woods, you don't want to stay at Manistee River Bridge. If nothing else the fact that it is located across from a canoe livery should tell you something.

Instead find your way to Upper Manistee River because this far upstream there is less development along the river and far less traffic on it. The campground is more of the wooded setting you expect up north and there's no M-72, a virtual Interstate with travelers during the summer, 50 yards from your trailer.

Directions: From M-72, turn north on Manistee River Road, a dirt road that is reached from Graying right before you cross the river. Follow it 6 miles to County Road 612, turn west, cross the river and then turn south (left) on Goose Creek Road where the campground is posted. The entrance is a mile south.

The quickest way to reach the campground from I-75 is to skip Grayling all together and depart at Frederic (exit 264) and head west on CR 612.

Campground: Upper Manistee River has 30 vehicle sites on two loops situated in a pine forest with an undergrowth of ferns. The sites are well spread out and a few are along the bank above the river but not within view of the water. There are also 20 more group and walk-in sites in an area lightly forested with little undergrowth. This is a very pleasant section, well-worth the short walk in if you have a tent. Many sites are along the edge of the bank with a nice view of the Manistee gently flowing through a grassy area. Facilities include vault toilets, hand pumps for water, tables and fire rings.

Fishing: The upper Manistee is a popular fly fishing area for rainbow and brown trout. The river has been stabilized in many areas while log railings have been constructed along the banks in the campground. This far upstream the Manistee is 15-20 yards wide and with more than enough width to cast a fly rod at the raising rings. Most of the stream is less than four-feet deep, and can be easily waded though you might encounter a few deep holes in this area.

Canoeing: Upper Manistee has a canoe landing within its group sites along with canoe racks. Another canoe landing is situated just up river at the CR 612 bridge. From the county road it is an 18-mile paddle or four-hour trip to Manistee River Bridge Campground. The next state forest campground is CCC Campground, another 30 miles down stream. Canoes can be rented from *Long's Canoes* (517-348-7224) and *Shel-Haven* (517-348-2158), the livery on the river at M-72.

A young canoeist ready to go.

Season: Normally you can obtain a vehicle site and surely a walk-in at this campground even on the weekends. Just keep in mind that can change quickly if a large group of paddlers passes through.

55

SHUPAC LAKE
AU SABLE STATE FOREST

Region: Lake Huron
Nearest Community: Lovells
Sites: 30   **Reservations:** No
Fee: $6
Information: Mio DNR Office (517) 826-3211

Shupac Lake is a scenic body of water and a quiet one by law. Special regulations prevent high-speed boating while the limited number of cottages, mostly restricted to the southeast shoreline, allow the campers on the northwest corner to enjoy a little solitude in the woods.

The state forest campground is a long-time haven for trout fishermen who either take to the nearby North Branch of the Au Sable or fish Shupac Lake itself, which is stocked annually with rainbow trout.

But you don't have to be a fly fisher to enjoy this rustic facility. Practically all the campgrounds have a view of the water, the beach is sandy, the swimming excellent, and there is even a perch fishery to entertain those anglers not interested in tossing around feathers on a hook.

Directions: From I-75, depart at exit 264 and head east. In eight miles you pass the posted side road to Jones Lake State Forest Campground at which point County Road 612 begins curving its way to the village of Lovells. But just before crossing the North Branch into town, you turn north onto Twin Bridge Road and in 2 miles reach the posted entrance to the campground.

Campground: Shupac has 30 sites located on a long loop with almost every one of them on the edge of a bluff overlooking the lake. Situated in a forest of predominantly oak with moderate undergrowth, the sites are well spread out and secluded from each other and many feature their own log staircase leading down to the water. The northern half of the loop is especially scenic as you look out over a small, undeveloped bay at the north end of the lake. Tables, fire grills, a hand pump for water, and vault toilets are found along the loop.

A fly fishermen on the Au Sable River system.

Day-use Facilities: A small picnic area with a few tables is located at the south end of the campground and features a narrow beach of sorts next to the boat launch. No marked swimming area but the water is extremely clear and the sandy bottom gently slopes into the lake.

Fishing: There is a cement ramp in the day-use area with a large parking area, attesting to the popularity of the lake to anglers. Boating regulations include a ban on water skiing and "no high speed boating" which most locals interpret as no wake. The deep lake is stocked annually with rainbow trout but also supports perch and a bass fishery.

Just before entering the campground, you cross Twin Bridge, an access point for fly fishermen entering the North Branch of the Au Sable. This is a Quality Fishing Area, meaning artificial flies only. The daily limit is six trout of which brook trout have to be a minimum eight inches, all others 10 inches. The North Branch fishery has long considered one of Michigan's blue ribbon trout streams but, unfortunately, has suffered in recent years. Still it attracts steady pressure and fly shops in Lovells will be able to assist interested anglers with fly patterns and other access points.

Season: Occasionally this state forest campground can fill on a mid-summer weekend but usually a site can be obtained throughout the summer.

56

D.H. DAY
SLEEPING BEAR DUNES
NATIONAL LAKESHORE

Region: Northwest
Nearest Community: Glen Arbor
Sites: 88   **Reservations:** No
Fee: $8
Information: Park headquarters (616) 326-5134

D.H. Day was the first chairmen of the State Park Commission that, in the wake of a growing number of motorized campers in the 1920s, had the task of setting up Michigan's present system. Ironically, Day's name is attached today to one of the most popular National Park Service facilities in Michigan and not a state park.

But the conservationist would hardly mind. D.H. Day Campground in Sleeping Bear Dunes National Lakeshore is an excellent facility, featuring somewhat secluded sites despite its size, nightly ranger programs during the summer and one of the finest beaches in a state known for great beaches.

All of this plus the popularity of the dunes themselves makes D.H. Day Campground one of the busiest public facilities in Michigan. To put it simply, it's filled nightly from June through Labor Day. Either show up early in the morning or keep heading north. There's rarely an open site for afternoon arrivals.

Directions: From the park headquarters on the corner of M-72 and M-22 in Empire, head north on M-22 and veer left onto M-119. Within five miles you'll pass the Dune Climb and in another mile curve right towards the town of Glen Arbor. Before reaching the town you'll pass the posted entrance to the campground.

Campground: D.H. Day has 88 sites along one large loop and two smaller ones. Located right off Sleeping Bear Bay, the campground features a rolling terrain well forested in pine and hardwoods giving most sites a bit of seclusion despite the number of tents and trailers they pack in here. None of them are within sight of Lake Michigan but four sites, 58-

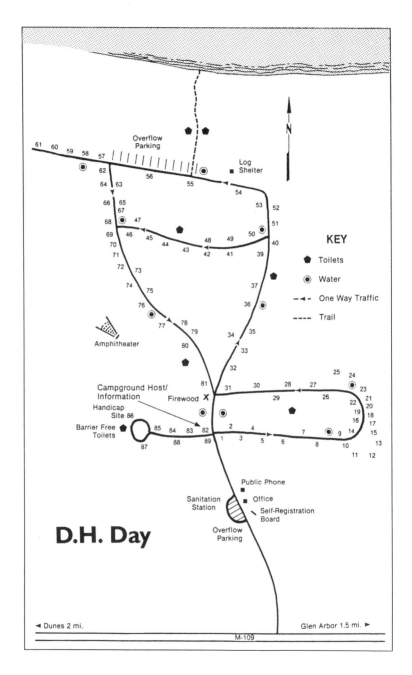

KEY

🔶 Toilets

◉ Water

◄ One Way Traffic

---- Trail

D.H. Day

◄ Dunes 2 mi.

Glen Arbor 1.5 mi. ►

M-109

138

61, are off by themselves on a dead end spur.

Amenities include fire rings, tables, vault toilets and hand pumps for water. Although this is a rustic facility there is also a sanitation station for recreational vehicles along with pay phones and a firewood concession that is open from 7-9 p.m. nightly. Site 86 is a handicapped site and located next to a barrier-free vault toilet.

Day-use Facilities: In the back of the campground is limited parking for day-use visitors located next to a log cabin. From here a path leads north to quickly emerge at an incredible stretch of Lake Michigan beach. The sand is as fine as sugar, the water is shallow and turquoise in color and the view from your towel is a panorama second to none on any Michigan shoreline. To the west you can see Sleeping Bear Dune, to the east Pyramid Point raising straight out of the lake and due north are the Manitou Islands with the lighthouse on South Manitou Island easily visible on a clear day. The boat traffic, from freighters and sailboats to the Manitou Islands ferries, adds yet another pleasant dimension to this spot.

There is also an amphitheater, complete with screen in a wooded hollow on the west side of the campground. The National Park Service offers a variety of free interpretive programs throughout the summer and a schedule is posted at the entrance to the amphitheater.

Hiking: Although there are no trails that depart from the camp-ground, the northern portion of the Sleeping Bears Dunes abounds with hiking opportunities. The closest and one of the most popular in the park is the *Dunes Trail* located a mile south on M-119. It begins with the steep Dune Climb and then continues another 1.5 miles out to Lake Michigan. Round trip is a good 4 miles and of moderate difficulty. West beyond the Maritime Museum on County Road 209 is *Sleeping Bear Point Trail*, a 2.8-mile loop with much of it through loose sand of moderately rolling dunes. A short spur at the beginning leads to Lake Michigan.

Alligator Hill Trail is located south of the campground on Stocking Road and consists of three loops of 2.5 miles each. These trails are better for Nordic skiers than hikers as the views are now obscured by trees. Not true with *Pyramid Point Trail,* located 3.7 miles north of Glen Arbor via Port Oneida Road north then Basch Road east. The 2.6-loop loop includes a spur to a high point on Pyramid Point with a spectacular view of Lake Michigan. The bluff is so steep that hang gliders occasionally take off from the overlook.

Nearby Attractions: Along with the renowned Dune Climb, other attractions in this end of the park include the Maritime Museum

The Dune Climb at Sleeping Bear Dunes National Lakeshore.

along County Road 209. The renovated Lifesaving Station features displays and exhibits on the U.S Lifesaving Service, which predated the U.S. Coast Guard, and a fascinating interpretive program on how they used a breeches buoy and a cannon to save distressed sailors. Pierce Stocking Drive is an 8-mile, one-way loop that you cover in your car or on a bicycle. Along the way there is a covered bridge, interpretive posts and several scenic overlooks.

Season: The campground is managed by a host in site 82 from June through Labor Day. No reservations are accepted as all sites are handed out on a first-come-first-serve basis. D.H. Day is filled daily during the summer, usually by 1 p.m. Plan on camping nearby the night before and arriving between 8-9 a.m. to stake out sites that are vacated. Pitch your tent and fill out a form, then you can continue your tour of Sleeping Bear Dunes.

LEELANAU
STATE PARK

Region: Northwest
Nearest Community: Northport
Sites: 52   **Reservations:** Yes
Fee: $6 plus a vehicle entry permit
Information: Park headquarters (616) 386-5422

The campground at Leelanau State Park may be rustic but it's popular. Despite the lack of modern restrooms, showers or electrical hook-ups, the facility fills up daily throughout most of the summer due to both its location and scenery.

The campground is situated at the very top of the Leelanau Peninsula, providing splendid views of where the waters of Grand Traverse Bay merge with those of Lake Michigan. Lakeside sites are plentiful, while a short walk away is Grand Traverse Lighthouse that has been converted into an interesting museum. There is no beach at the tip but an enjoyable afternoon can be spent hiking into the park's separate Cathead Bay-area for sand and surf.

Directions: The state park is split between two sections with the campground at the tip, 8 miles north of Northport on County Road 629. Access to Cathead Bay is 4 miles north of the town and is reached by turning off CR 629 onto Densmore Road and heading west to the trailhead at the end.

Campground: There are 52 sites along several loops at the tip of the peninsula. Most are situated in an area forested in pines and are not grouped together as tightly as the average state park. Almost half of them have a view of the water and 11 sites are right on the shore, combining a little shade and easy access to Lake Michigan. These sites are very sandy but the beach is rocky, poor for swimming but great for Petoskey stone hunters.

The sites have tables and fire rings while nearby are vault toilets and hand pumps for water. Also located within the campground are the remnants of the first lighthouse on the point (1853-1857) in a fenced-in area next to site 47.

Grand Traverse Lighthouse at Leelanau State Park.

Day-use Facilities: Away from the shore is an open grassy area with play equipment, shelter, and picnic tables, pedestal grills. Nearby is Grand Traverse Lighthouse, which was built in 1916 as the most recent in a series of lighthouses that have been guiding ships around the peninsula since 1852. Inside there are displays in several rooms on the first floor while a staircase winds to the top of the tower for an immense view.

Hiking: Most of the 1,253-acre park lies in an undeveloped section around Cathead Bay. Winding through this area of wooded dunes is a 6-mile network of trails used by both hikers in the summer and Nordic skiers in the winter. There are several loops of various lengths within the area but those intent on reaching the beautiful sandy beach along Cathead Bay should follow the *Lake Michigan Trail*. The 1.5-mile loop passes a short spur that emerges from trees, crosses several low dunes and ends on a beautiful shoreline.

Season: Leelanau State Park is open May through October and fills every day from the Fourth of July holiday to Labor Day. The park reserves 32 sites in advance and hands out the rest on a first-come-first-serve basis. Whatever site opens up is usually claimed by 9:30 a.m. Make reservations if possible for this is a very popular campground.

58

ARBUTUS LAKE NO. 4
PERE MARQUETTE STATE FOREST

Region: Northwest
Nearest Community: Traverse City
Sites: 38   **Reservations:** No
Fee: $6
Information: Cadillac DNR office (616) 775-9727

A mere 10 miles south of Traverse City is Arbutus Lake No. 4 State Forest Campground, overlooking the shores of this chain of five lakes. The facility is no more than a 15-minute drive from downtown but a world away as far as this bustling tourist town is concerned.

The campground is unique, built on the side of a hill with many of the small sites terraced above the water, while the lakes themselves are a haven of boating and fishing activities during the summer. There is also a beach and even a pathway. The only sign that Traverse City is on your doorstep is the lack of empty sites on the weekends.

Directions: From Traverse City head south on Garfield Road (M-611), then turn east (left) on Hobbs Highway. The road is a scenic and hilly drive around Arbutus Lake No. 5 before arriving at the junction with Arbutus Road. Head north (left) and in two miles a sign will direct you to turn west on a gravel road to the campground entrance.

Campground: This delightful campground is basically a loop around a prominent hill raising straight above the lake. Many of the sites can only be reached via a stairway from where you park your vehicle while others are situated on the edge of the bluff above the water and have been terraced to make room for a tent. The view of waves lapping against the shore almost straight below makes these the first sites to be picked.

Most of the hill is forested in maples and other hardwoods but a few sites on the back site are in a small clearing. All of them have a table, and fire ring while nearby are vault toilets and hand pump for water. Needless to say, much of the campground and certainly the most scenic sites are not conducive to recreation vehicles of any size.

Day-use Facilities: The campground features a grassy area leading to a thin beach and a marked swimming area that is shallow with a sandy bottom. Also in the area are a few tables, vault toilets and a hand pump.

Boating: The campground lies on the fourth lake of a five-lake chain, that is popular with boaters. To the north is Arbutus Lake No. 5 while to the south lie No. 1, 2 and 3. An East Bay Township ordinance limits high speed boating and water skiing on Lakes No. 2, 3 and 4 from 10 a.m. until 6:30 p.m. each day and bans it entirely on Lakes No. 1 and 5.

There is an unimproved, dirt boat launch in the day-use area of the campground along with parking for four maybe five vehicles.

Fishing: Lake No. 4 has a lily-pad covered bay next to the campground and shore anglers can toss worms and crickets along its edges for bluegill, sunfish and other panfish. The chain as a whole has a mixed bag of a fishery including yellow perch, northern pike and black crappie. It is best fished for bass, with some largemouth exceeding 20 inches in length, and bluegill.

Hiking: The *Chandler Lake Pathway* departs from near the day-use area and is a loop that crosses a dirt road to the campground before passing a picnic area on Chandler Lake at the halfway point. The loop is a 1.5-mile hike through a wooded and hilly area while a spur shortens it to a 1-mile trek before reaching the lake.

Season: The campground is not managed during the summer and all sites are available on a first-come-first serve basis. Arbutus Lake's close proximity to Traverse City makes it a popular designation and often the campground will be filled on the weekends in July and August.

59

LAKE DUBONNET
PERE MARQUETTE STATE FOREST

Region: Northwest
Nearest Community: Interlochen
Sites: 50   **Reservations:** No
Fee: $6
Information: Cadillac DNR Office (616) 775-9727

Lake Dubonnet is one of the largest state forest facilities in Michigan but come evening it can still be an enchanting place. A pair of loons nest here and after nightfall their erie laugh can often be heard from every site. That wild call along with the fact that the lake, with the exception of one cottage, is totally undeveloped, gives the campground a Northwoods touch, a rarity for any facility this big and this close to Traverse City.

The lake was actually created in 1956 when a stream was dammed to improve fishing and waterfowl habitat. As a result the size of the lake nearly doubled as two lakes were merged into one by the rising water. Across the inlet on its north side is a rustic campground, built for hikers and equestrians following the Shore-To-Shore Trail that passes through the area. Lake Dubonnet also has a handicapped site located near a fishing pier that is accessible to the physically impaired but enjoyed by all who like tossing a fishing line from shore.

Directions: From Traverse City head west on US-31 and in 14 miles, or a mile past M-137, turn north on Wildwood Road.

Campground: The facility has four loops of 50 sites. But don't despair at its size. The sites are well spread in an area forested with a mix of maple, oak, aspen and even some paper birch with a good growth of undercover. Sites have tables, fire rings and angled spurs that make pulling an RV in and out easy. There are also hand pumps for water and vault toilets. None of the sites are directly on the lake but a handful are on the edge of the bluff overlooking the lake while a few more are located along an inlet. A special handicapped site is located in the second loop and includes a special table and a handicapped accessible vault toilet nearby.

Fishing: There is an improved boat launch with a cement ramp

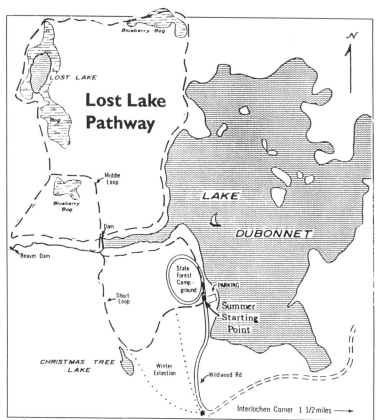

and parking for a handful of cars near the entrance of the campground. Lake Dubonnet has bass and northern pike populations but is best for bluegill and other panfish, especially from the fishing pier that extends out at the mouth of the inlet that borders the campground. This close to shore the fish tend to be stunted but children still find them fun to catch.

Hiking: The *Lost Lake Pathway* begins in the campground near the handicapped site and includes several loops. At one point it was set up with interpretive markers but most of them are now gone and the path itself can be difficult to follow in places due primarily to forest roads and other trails passing through the area. The loop, a 5.5-mile trek passes some interesting bogs, including one that surrounds Lost Lake.

Season: Lake Dubonnet can become busy during the height of the summer camping season but it is rare for this campground to fill-up, even on a weekend.

60

GREEN LAKE
INTERLOCHEN STATE PARK

Region: Northwest
Nearest Community: Interlochen
Sites: 33   **Reservations:** Yes
Fee: $6 plus a vehicle entry permit
Information: Park headquarters (616) 276-9511

Bach, Beethoven and a bass at the end of your line; only at Interlochen State Park. The 200-acre state park is Michigan's second oldest, preserved in 1917 after it's virgin stand of white pine had somehow escaped the swinging axes of lumberjacks. But today it's best known as the park next to renowned Interlochen National Music Camp. This might be the only place in Michigan where you bed down to classical music as opposed to campfire songs from the site next door.

Interlochen is actually a thin strip of land between two lakes, Duck and Green, and features almost a mile of shoreline as well as its towering pines. Along Duck Lake is a modern campground and 500 of the park's 576 sites. My favorite, however, is the rustic campground along Green Lake where the sites are further apart and more private than those across the road. Green Lake is also one of the few rustic campgrounds where you can make reservations.

Directions: Interlochen is located 15 miles southwest of Traverse City and is reached from the resort town by heading south on US-31. The park's entrance is on M-137, 3 miles south of US-31.

Campground: Green Lake has two loops of 76 rustic sites with tables, fire rings, vault toilets and hand pumps for water. Many of them are along the edge of a shoreline bluff with an excellent view of the water. All of them are spread out in a well forested area that is generally a little cooler at night than the other campground. You give up a shower but you get a lot more privacy in return. The wood lot is near the modern campground on the other side of M-137 and open daily from 5-9 p.m. during the summer.

Day-use Facilities: The park's picnic and swimming areas are on

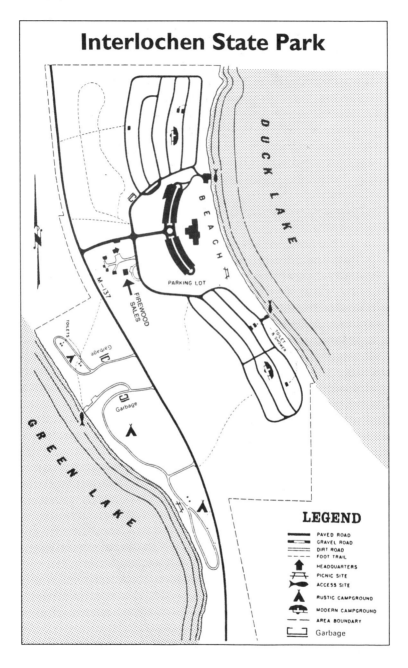

Interlochen State Park

LEGEND

PAVED ROAD
GRAVEL ROAD
DIRT ROAD
FOOT TRAIL
HEADQUARTERS
PICNIC SITE
ACCESS SITE
RUSTIC CAMPGROUND
MODERN CAMPGROUND
AREA BOUNDARY
Garbage

Duck Lake where you'll find a wide sandy beach, a designated swimming area, tables and a shelter that can be rented. There is also a boat rental concession that has rowboats on both Duck and Green Lake and is open daily Memorial Day through Labor Day, 8 a.m. to 9 p.m.

Fishing: There is considerable fishing activity in the park as both lakes are considered excellent smallmouth bass waters with a number of tournaments staged here throughout the summer. Green Lake, however, has a wider variety of fish including perch, northern pike and brown trout as well as panfish. The park maintains three improved boat launches with cement slabs. Two are at the end of each loop in the modern campground and the third is in the rustic campground.

Hiking: The only path is *Pines Nature Trail*, a mile-long loop that winds through the towering stand of white pine. It begins from the south loop of the modern campground and has 16 interpretive stops.

Season: The campground is open from mid-April to mid-October. The modern campground is filled weekends and often by Thursday from late June through late August. The demand on Green Lake is not nearly as great but it also fills most summer weekends. Either arrive in mid-week or reserve a site in advance.

61

GUERNSEY LAKE
PERE MARQUETTE STATE FOREST

Region: Northwest
Nearest Community: Kalkaska
Sites: 30   **Reservations:** No
Fee: $6
Information: Kalkaska DNR Office (616) 258-2711

Located just eight miles west of Kalkaska, Guernsey Lake is a state forest campground overlooking an undeveloped lake with lots of opportunities for fishing, hiking, even an overnight backpacking adventure if you wish.

Small lakes abound in this part of the Pere Marquette State Forest. Surrounding the entrance of the campground are Little Guernsey Lakes, three small bodies of water within view of Campground Road. Or the more adventurous can explore, fish or even camp along Sand Lakes, five lakes in the middle of the Sand Lakes Quiet Head which has a trailhead in the state forest campground.

Directions: You can reach the campground from County Road 660 just south of Traverse City but once on Scenic Drive you'll find it a very rough ride. A smoother route is from Kalkaska where you turn west on Island Lake Road just north of the McDonalds on US-131. Within 5.5 miles you pass Island Lake then veer to the left on the dirt road and follow it 1.5 miles to Campground Road. Although Campground Road is not posted, there is a state forest campground symbol here. Turn south (left) and the campground entrance is reached in a mile.

Campground: Guernsey Lake has a pair of loops with 12 sites on one and 18 on the other. All sites are situated on a bluff above the lake with stairways and log fences leading down to the water in several places. Forested in oak, maple and red pine, the sites are shaded and well spaced but not totally secluded from each other. A few on the large loop have a glimpse of the lake but none directly overlook the water. Facilities include tables and fire rings, though many are missing, as well as a hand pump for water and vault toilets.

Day-use Facilities: On a fenced-in bluff overlooking the lake near the boat launch is a pleasant, well shaded spot that, unfortunately, lacks most of its tables and grills.

Fishing: The campground has an unimproved boat launch directly on Guernsey Lake with additional parking for a handful of vehicles and rigs. Guernsey is stocked annually with rainbow and brown trout but during the summer most anglers end up catching bluegill and, to a much lesser degree, bass. There is a "No Wake" regulation on Guernsey and the lake can easily be fished from a canoe or rowboat.

Nearby are the Little Guernsey Lakes and the only one on the west side of Campground Road is the largest and most accessible for those with a hand-carried boat or canoe. Almost directly across from the campground entrance is an unmarked two-track that leads back to another Little Guernsey Lake. Finally, walk-in fishing opportunities exist in the Sand Lakes Quiet Lake. Sand Lake No. 3 is often fished for bass and panfish while Sand Lake No. 2 is another designated trout lake.

Hiking: *Sand Lakes Quiet Area* is a 2,500-acre preserve that borders Guernsey Lake to the west with a trailhead and parking area in the campground. The foot trail within the quiet area is basically an 8-mile loop with most of the lakes clustered on the west side. It is a 2.6-mile trek to the backcountry campsite on Sand Lake No. 1 if you hike the north half of the loop and 4.4-mile walk along the southern half.

Season: On a July or August weekend this campground could be more than two-thirds full but it is rare to arrive here and not find at least one open site.

62

FISHERMAN'S ISLAND
STATE PARK

Region: Northwest
Nearest Community: Charlevoix
Sites: 90   **Reservations:** Yes
Fee: $6 plus a vehicle entry permit
Information: Park headquarters (616) 547-6641

Half hidden from US-31 south of Charlevoix is Fisherman's Island State Park and those who know about it often associate it with Petoskey stones. The 2,678-acre park is a haven during the summer for lapidaries and others looking for the state stone, a fossil with the honeycomb design.

But the park also features some of the most beautiful stretches of beach in this crowded corner of Lake Michigan. And because of the beach, Fisherman's Island also has some of the nicest rustic sites in the state park system, spots where you can pitch your tent a few feet from the lapping waters of the Great Lake and be so secluded from the rest of the park you practically have a private beach of your own. They're hard to obtain during the summer but they are well worth waiting for a day or two.

Directions: From Charlevoix head 5 miles south on US-31 and then west on Bell Bay Road. The park is posted on US-31 and its entrance is 2.5 miles along Bell Bay Road.

Campground: The park has 90 rustic sites with tables and fire rings on three separate loops and along Lake Michigan. The loops are well forested in a mix of hardwoods, especially paper birch, and the sites are well secluded from each other. Particularly the third and newest loop, sites 41-90, where there are even a few tent sites tucked up a hill and reached via a short stairway.

But the most popular sites and some of the most scenic in the Lower

Swimmers enjoy the beach at Fisherman's Island State Park.

Peninsula are those along the beach. Fisherman's Island has 15 sites (9 and 27-40) right off the park drive where your tent or RV is on a sandy beach and within view of Lake Michigan. They are well spread and for the most part secluded from each other. Some are close to the road but most are tucked away from the asphalt with a beach of their own; what a deal for $6 a night. The loops have vault toilets and hand pumps for water.

Day-use Facilities: The picnic area is located at the south end of the park drive and includes parking, vault toilets, tables, pedestal grills and access to a beach. A wooden foot bridge crosses Inwood Creek and from here you can walk over a low dune to more beautiful stretches of sand and surf, totally undeveloped as far as you can see and crowned by Fisherman's Island just offshore. It's a beautiful setting for swimming or sunbathing.

Hiking: The park has a four-mile network of trails which basically form a path from the contact station to the day-use area with a few spurs, including one to the last loop of sites. There is a parking area near the contact station and from the northern trailhead it's a walk of 3.2 miles to the day-use area and a trek of 2 miles to the last loop of campsites. The first portion of the trail is a foot path that remains in the woods as you cross McGeach Creek. But eventually it merges into an old farm road and passes through clearings and even an old apple orchard with the trees still bearing fruit. Here you can find some excellent berry patches, especially blackberries.

Fishing: There is no boat launch within the park and fishing is limited to river angling for steelhead and salmon near the mouths of McGeach and Whiskey Creek with the best runs taking place in March and May. Whiskey Creek is reached from a two-track road out of Norway Township Park.

Season: With 90 sites, there are usually openings in midweek and often a few on the weekends during the summer. You can not reserve the beach sites and don't even plan on getting one when you show up. Most people camp along the loops the first night and then arrive at the contact station at 8 a.m. the next day for a site transfer to the beach. You have a better chance Sunday and Monday for a beach site than the rest of the week. Call the park headquarters (616-547-6641) for a reservation. The park is open May through October and up to 70 percent of the sites can be reserved in advance.

63

PICKEREL LAKE
PIGEON RIVER COUNTRY STATE FOREST

Region: Northwest
Nearest Community: Vanderbilt
Sites: 39   **Reservations:** No
Fee: $6
Information: Pigeon River Country (517) 983-4101

How rugged is Pigeon River State Forest? Just up Pickerel Lake Road is a scenic pull-off with a view of nothing but forested ridges and hills for miles. From there it's a straight drop down to the campground that will have your children gripping the back of your seat and you worried about the trailer. That's how rugged.

The state forest comprises almost 98,000 contiguous acres and includes seven campgrounds, 60 miles of foot trails, 27 miles of horse trails and the largest elk herd east of the Mississippi River. Of the campgrounds Pickerel is on the largest, most popular and, from an angler's point of view, the nicest lake.

Directions: From I-75 depart at exit 290 and in the town of Vanderbilt head west on Sturgeon Valley Road. Ten miles from Vanderbilt turn north (left) on Pickerel Lake Road to reach the posted campground entrance in two miles.

Pigeon River Country State Forest elk.

Campground: The north shore of Pickerel Lake was a camp for the Civilian Conservation Corps during the 1930s, the reason, no doubt, for the lightly forested campground you find today. There are enough trees for shade but not enough to isolate the sites for the kind privacy you find in most state forest campgrounds. Three loops contain 39 sites but tables and fire rings are lacking on many of them. None of the sites are on the water or even within view of the lake. Vault toilets and hand pumps for water are in each loop.

Day-use Facilities: There is no beach along the lake but a grassy area serves as one while the water here is shallow for 30 or 40 yards with a fine gravel bottom.

Fishing: There is an unimproved boat launch with limited parking for a handful of vehicles. Pickerel Lake is completely undeveloped and has a ban on boat motors other than electric. The lake is stocked on a regular basis with rainbow trout while many anglers target it for bass and bluegill.

Hiking: Passing the boat launch area is *Pickerel Lake Pathway*, a 2-mile hike that circles the lake. It's marked by blue blazes and most of it stays within sight of the water.

Elk Watching: Within the state forest are several posted elk viewing areas, including one just east Pickerel Lake Road on Sturgeon Valley Road. The bugle season, when the bulls emerge from the forests to call in their harem, is best from mid-September through October.

Season: With the exception of Fourth of July and when Gaylord stages its Alpenfest celebration, it is rare for this campground to fill up during the summer and even if it did, there are several more nearby.

64

PIGEON RIVER

PIGEON RIVER COUNTRY STATE FOREST

Region: Northwest
Nearest Community: Vanderbilt
Sites: 19   **Reservations:** No
Fee: $6
Information: State forest headquarters (517) 983-4101

Within the Pigeon River County State Forest, a tract of more than 98,000 acres east of Vanderbilt, are seven rustic campgrounds. With the exception of Pickerel Lake, all are small, out-of-the-way campgrounds in this rugged corner of the Lower Peninsula, home of the largest elk herd east of the Mississippi.

This includes Pigeon River where it's easy to get turned around trying to find the rustic campground...or trying to find your way back to the highway. But that is also the nicest feature. If you camp to escape into the woods, Pigeon River is a good destination, a miles-from-anywhere campground with little more than fire rings, tables and vault toilets.

Directions: The campground is 13 miles east of Vanderbilt and reached by departing I-75 at exit 290. In downtown Vanderbilt turn east (left) on Sturgeon Valley Road and in 10 miles you will enter the state forest. After crossing the Pigeon River, then turn north (left) on Osmond Road to arrive at the new forest headquarters, an impressive log lodge. Stop and get a map and then continue north on Osmond Road as it curves and winds its way past the posted entrance to the campground.

Campground: Pigeon River is a single, one-way loop of 19 well-secluded sites spread out along the forested banks of its namesake river. Most of the sites are out of view of the water but a few are right on the bank, including site 19 that overlooks a river bridge and is a scenic spot to park a RV. Facilities include tables and fire rings at most sites and vault toilets and a hand pump for water.

Day-use Facilities: A small, overgrown picnic area is at the south end of the loop with but a table and a grill. The popular spot to picnic, however, is at the bridge. Here the river has been dammed up slightly to

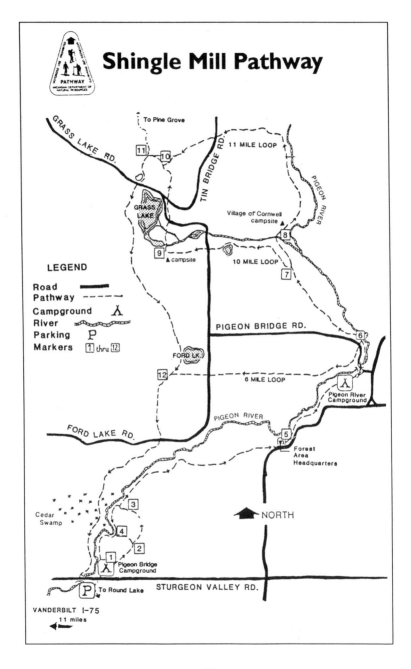

Shingle Mill Pathway

RVers making camp at a state forest campground.

create a pool for wading and cooling off while open grassy banks lend themselves well to laying out in the sun on a hot August afternoon.

Fishing: Although many say the Pigeon is not supporting the trout populations it did a decade ago, the river still attracts a fair number of anglers. In June, half the sites here will have a pair of waders drying from a branch in mid-afternoon. In the campground the river is 30-40 feet wide and rarely more than 4 feet deep, making it easy wading with the exception of a few deep holes. Both brown and brook trout inhabit the Pigeon though you're most likely to catch a brown.

Tubing: Not much canoeing activity but tubing seems popular, so popular that the campground hosts rent out a few truck tubes.

Hiking: The *Shingle Mill Pathway* passes through the campground and crosses the bridge over the Pigeon River here. The pathway is a series of loops that begins at Pigeon Bridge Campground on Sturgeon Valley Road and follows the river much of the way. The hike from the campground to Sturgeon Valley Road and back would be a six-mile trek.

Season: This campground is not nearly as poplar as the smaller Pigeon Bridge Campground or Pickerel Lake. On an average July weekend it will be less than half filled. A campground host manages the facility during the summer.

65

BIG BEAR LAKE
MACKINAW STATE FOREST

Region: Northwest
Nearest Community: Vienna Corners
Sites: 43   **Reservations:** No
Fee: $6
Information: Gaylord DNR Office (616) 732-3541

The main campground on Big Bear Lake lacks a boat ramp as well as the privacy usually associated with state forest campgrounds. But it does have one feature most other units would be hard pressed to match; a beautiful beach only a few steps from your site.

The clear water of the lake combined with the sandy strip at its north shore is no doubt the reason for its popularity. This is one of the few state forest units that can easily be filled on any summer weekend. Big Bear also features an interesting foot trail, an opportunity to watch beavers and moderately good fishing for several species including walleye and pike.

Directions: From I-75 depart at exit 282 and head east through downtown Gaylord on M-32. The hamlet of Vienna Corners is reached in 19 miles where you turn south on County Road F-01 for 1.2 miles and then west on Little Bear Road to the posted entrance of the campground.

Campground: There are two loops on the lake each with their own entrance off Little Bear Lake Road. The main loop has 30 sites on the northeast corner of the lake with 15 of them overlooking the beach and lake. The area is lightly forested in hardwoods with little undergrowth; thus the lack of isolation from your neighbors.

The smaller loop is on the northwest corner of the lake and has 13 sites in a thicker forest and heavier brush. Not only is there more privacy but four of the sites are situated on a low bluff above the water with a scenic view of the entire lake. Both loops have tables, fire rings, hand pumps for water and vault toilets.

Day-use Facilities: A small picnic area is situated along the beach in the main campground and has tables, pedestal grills and limited parking. The beach is nice, the reason this loop fills up first, and there is a large

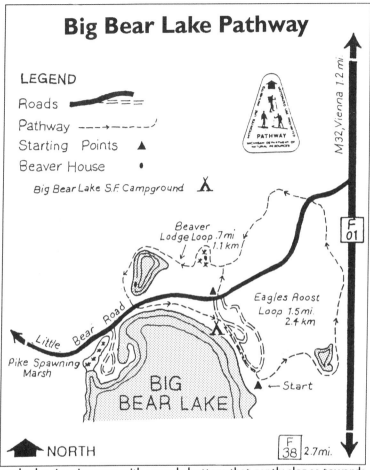

Big Bear Lake Pathway

LEGEND

Roads

Pathway

Starting Points ▲

Beaver House •

Big Bear Lake S.F. Campground

PATHWAY

M32, Vienna 1.2 mi.

F 01

Beaver Lodge Loop .7 mi / 1.1 km

Eagles Roost Loop 1.5 mi. 2.4 km

Little Bear Road

Pike Spawning Marsh

BIG BEAR LAKE

Start

NORTH

F 38 | 2.7 mi.

marked swimming area with a sandy bottom that gently slopes towards the deeper sections of the lake.

Fishing: The campground lacks a cement ramp but hand carried boats are easy to launch from either loop and a few campers even use their trailers along the shore to put in something larger. Big Bear is primarily known as a good walleye fishery with most anglers working the drop-offs with jigs and crawlers to entice the popular gamefish. There is also northern pike as the small loop borders a pike spawning marsh, and of course, bluegill, pumpkinseed and other panfish. One of the best places for children to fish for bluegills from the shore is the sandy spit that

Pitcher plants seen along the Big Bear Lake Pathway.

extends out from the small loop.

Hiking: The *Big Bear Lake Pathway* is a 2.2-mile trail divided into two loops. Some sections are difficult to follow but it's hard to get lost because you are never very far from a road. One posted trailhead is near the picnic area in the large loop and from here it is a half-mile walk to reach a pond where there is usually one or two active beaver lodges.

The trail also departs west from the opposite end of the large loop and from here you skirt the lake, cross Little Bear Lake Road and on the other side come to a much bigger pond with more beaver activity. Search this area for both wild berries and pink lady slipper orchids.

Season: This campground is popular and from mid-July to mid-August you might have difficulty getting a site on a Saturday afternoon or even Friday evening. I've been here when it has even been filled in mid-week but that is rare.

66

MAPLE BAY
MACKINAW STATE FOREST

Region: The Tip
Nearest Community: Brutus
Sites: 36   **Reservations:** No
Fee: $6
Information: Gaylord DNR office (517) 732-3541

Burt Lake is a busy and heavily developed lake as evident from the line of docks just outside this campground. Still the 17,120-acre lake is a beautiful body of water, especially on a calm morning when you can sit in the day-use area and enjoy that first cup of coffee while waiting for the sunrise over the east shore. And because of its immense size, there seems to be minimum conflict between anglers and those zipping across the surface in motor boats or jet skis.

There are two state campgrounds on the lake but my favorite has always been this state forest unit over the modern facility at Burt Lake State Park. Either one has an excellent beach and swimming area and both will be busy through the camping season.

Directions: From I-75, depart at exit 310 at Indian River and head west on M-68 as it curves around the southern end of Burt Lake and the entrance to the state park. In 11 miles you reach the junction with US-31 in the town of Alanson. Head north on US-31 and in 3 miles head east (right) on Brutus Road. In 3.5 miles you'll reached the posted entrance to Maple Bay.

Campground: Maple Bay is a three-lane loop with 36 sites and forested in hardwoods. Six sites on the outside overlook the day-use area and Maple Bay, receiving a nice breeze in the evening. The rest are in a forested area with heavy undergrowth. Though Maple Bay is not as secluded as most state forest campgrounds, it does offer far more privacy than the state park on the southeast corner.

Sites have tables and a fire ring and many feature a pull through spur, making them ideal for large RVs. Hand pumps and vault toilets are scattered throughout the loop. The two drawbacks in Maple Bay are that the low-lying areas between the sites can get buggy during a wet spell and the raccoons which are a nuisance here. Every bit of food should be locked in your car.

Day-use Facilities: Maple Bay features a sandy beach that, while not nearly as wide as the state park, still makes for a pleasant spot to spend a hot summer afternoon. There is a marked swimming area with a soft bottom that is knee-deep shallow for more than 50 yards, perfect for children to splash around. Bordering the beach in a shaded grassy strip are tables and pedestal grills but no playground equipment.

Boating: The campground has an improved boat launch with additional parking for a half dozen vehicles and trailers. Burt Lake is popular with boaters as it is part of the Inland Waterway, an historic 40-mile chain of four lakes and three rivers that was first used by the Indians as a safer and shorter alternative for paddling the Straits of Mackinac from Lake Michigan to Lake Huron. The route actually begins in Conway on Crooked Lake, 6 miles from Petoskey on Little Traverse Bay and ends with the Cheboygan River flowing into the Straits. Burt Lake is in the middle of the route.

Fishing: Burt Lake is one of the most heavily fished inland lakes in Michigan. It is regarded as an excellent walleye fishery and anglers are most productive with the gamefish from late May to mid-June and again in the fall. The lake, which is almost 10 miles long, also supports a good perch population as well as bass, rock bass, various panfish species and to a lesser degree northern pike. There are bait and tackle shops in Alanson.

Season: Despite its size, Maple Bay fills up often on the weekends in July and August and during mid-week still might have only a handful of sites open.

67

TOMAHAWK CREEK FLOODING
MACKINAW STATE FOREST

Region: Lake Huron
Nearest Community: Onaway
Sites: 35   **Reservations:** No
Fee: $6
Information: Alpena DNR Office (517) 785-4251

There are three campgrounds in this section of the Mackinaw State Forest and none of them more than a 10-minutes drive from each other. Shoepac Lake offers the best hiking opportunities with the interesting Sink Holes Pathway nearby and the High Country Pathway passing through the area. Tomahawk Lake by far has the best beach and swimming area as well as numerous sites that overlooks the undeveloped lake.

But Tomahawk Creek Flooding, at least the east side, has the most scenic views from the sites and the best fishery of the four bodies of water accessible here. Take you pick. I chose the Flooding but this far north chances are you will find a site in any of them.

Directions: From Atlanta, head north on M-33 for 15 miles then turn east (right) on Tomahawk Lake Highway, which is not highway at all but rather a rough dirt road. The West Unit is posted within a mile, the East Unit follows. Both Tomahawk Lake and Shoepac Lake are posted further east.

Campground: The newest of the three campgrounds in this noted karst (sinkhole) area, Tomahawk Creek Flooding is actually 35 sites split between two units with one on the east side of the lake and the other on the west. The campground was constructed in the early 1980s and its *East Unit* is by far the most scenic. The three loops are lightly forested in hardwoods and on a bluff enclosed by a log fence and overlooking the water. A handful have a spectacular view of not only the lake but the creek beyond and ridges in the distance. Most of the sites have tables and fire rings while vault toilets and a hand pump for water are located within each loop. Long stairways lead down from the edge of the bluff to the water below.

The *West Unit* is closer to the shoreline but has no sites directly on it. These loops are heavily forested and the sites are more secluded but the view is not nearly as good.

Day-Use Facilities: Head to Tomahawk Lake where you will find a small but nice beach that is terraced with logs and located in the middle of the campground.

Fishing: Both units of Tomahawk Creek Flooding have an improved boat launch with a cement ramp and additional parking for a handful of vehicles and rigs. Of the four lakes in the area, the Flooding is by far the best with a strong bluegill fishery and other panfish as well as largemouth bass. There is also a pike fishery but the northerns caught are generally under-sized. Like most floodings, there is a large number of deadheads, stumps and timber still standing, especially at the south end of the lake. Fishing pressure appears moderate to light through most of the summer.

Hiking: Just beyond the entrance to Shoepac Lake Campground is a posted trailhead to *Sinkholes Pathway*. The 2.4-mile loop is an easy to moderate hike around five sinkholes, huge depressions in the ground formed when limestone caves collapsed. The first is the most impressive and is reached only 10 minutes from the trailhead. Also passing through here is the *High Country Pathway*, a 50-mile, five to seven day loop that many people begin at Clear Lake State Park to the south on M-33.

Season: All three campgrounds are large and even though some loops are closed due to budget constraints, getting a site in any them is easy mid-week or even on the weekend.

68

OCQUEOC FALLS
MACKINAW STATE FOREST

Region: The Tip
Nearest Community: Ocqueoc
Sites: 14   **Reservations:** No
Fee: $6
Information: Gaylord DNR office (517) 732-3541

Although called Ocqueoc Falls State Forest Campground, the falls, the largest cascade and many say the only true one in the Lower Peninsula, is actually across the street in a day-use area of its own. Even without a view of the small waterfalls, this rustic campground is worth pulling into and can provide you a quiet and secluded site among pines and hardwoods overlooking the scenic river.

Directions: The falls and campground are just off M-68 on Ocqueoc Falls Highway, 10 miles northeast of Onaway or 11.5 miles west of Rogers City.

Campground: Ocqueoc Falls is a single loop of 14 sites, all of them near the river and a half dozen on the edge of the low bluff that towers directly above water. The sites are well separated and secluded from each other in a forest of red pine, paper birch and mixed hardwoods. There is tables and fire rings at most sites, but not all, and vault toilets and a hand pump for water in the campground.

Day-use Facilities: The posted entrance and paved parking area to Ocqueoc Falls Scenic Site are across the street from the campground. Opened from 8 a.m. to 10 p.m. the area has tables, pedestal grills and vault toilets. It's a short walk of 30 yards from the parking area to the river and falls. There is actually another set of falls off the Manistee River in the Lower Peninsula but Ocqueoc is definitely the most impressive. It descends six feet in a series of levels with one drop a particularly favorite for children to sit under on a hot summer day.

Fishing: The Ocqueoc River offers a fishery that ranges from warmwater species of pike and smallmouth bass in its upper sections where it flows through Barnhart Lake to salmon, brown trout and

A young camper enjoys the cooling waters of Ocqueoc Falls.

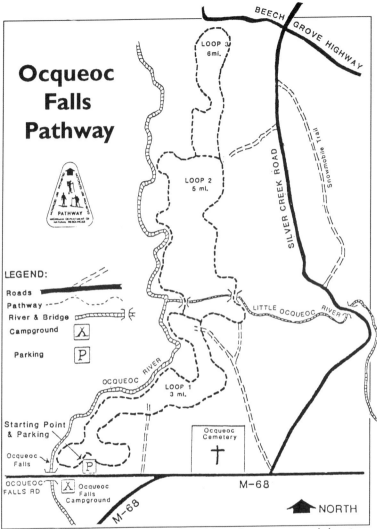

Ocqueoc Falls Pathway

LOOP 3
6 mi.

LOOP 2
5 mi.

BEECH GROVE HIGHWAY

SILVER CREEK ROAD

Snowmobile Trail

LEGEND:

Roads
Pathway
River & Bridge
Campground
Parking

LITTLE OCQUEOC RIVER

OCQUEOC RIVER

LOOP 1
3 mi.

Starting Point
& Parking

Ocqueoc
Falls

Ocqueoc
Cemetery

OCQUEOC
FALLS RD

Ocqueoc
Falls
Campground

M-68

M-68

NORTH

steelhead in its downstream stretches. Near the campground the river is 15-20 feet wide and can be easily waded in most places while just below the falls it's joined by the Little Ocqueoc River, one of two main tributaries and a noted brook trout stream. During the summer much of the Ocqueoc is not cold enough to hold trout and its heaviest fishing pressure is from steelheaders who arrive in the spring and fall for the annual run.

Hiking: *Ocqueoc Falls Pathway,* built in 1976 as a Bicentennial project, begins with a posted trailhead in the parking lot of the day-use area. The trail is designed to be used by both hikers and cross country skiers and consists of 3-mile, 5-mile and 6-mile loops. As far as hiking is concerned, the first loop is not only the shortest but the most scenic of the three.

Canoeing: The Ocqueoc River makes for a 30-mile canoe route that begins at an access site on Lake Emma off of County Road 634 and ends at its mouth on Lake Huron's Hammond Bay. You have to portage around the falls and other sections of this river can be challenging. Ocqueoc Falls is the only campground along the river.

Season: This is a lightly used facility that rarely fills up.

STATE PARK
RUSTIC CABINS

69

ROSTON CABIN
HOLLY RECREATION AREA

Region: Southeast
Nearest Community: Ortonville
Bunks: 6
Fee: $35 plus vehicle entry permit
Information: Park headquarters (313) 634-8811

In the early 1940s, a family named Roston drove north of Detroit until they had escaped all the trappings of the city and then built themselves a snug little log cabin on the edge of a pond. This was their weekend escape for the next 40 years, a quiet place to escape without having to drive halfway across the state.

And a funny thing happened along the way. Over the years urban sprawl seeped into northern Oakland County but the cabin always remained a quiet sanctuary thanks to Holly Recreation Area, the 7,800-acre state park unit that now surrounds it. Eventually the park obtained the log structure and today you can escape to Roston Cabin much like its original owners did nearly a half century ago. You don't have to drive up north, you don't even have to hike in as its private entrance with a gate and lock ensures you of a personal retreat into the woods.

Directions: The cabin is 25 miles north of Pontiac and reached by departing I-75 east onto Grange Hall Road (exit 101). Head east past Dixie Highway as well as the park headquarters on the south side of the road where you register and pick up the key. At this point Grange Hall Road takes a sharp curve north but park signs direct you straight onto McGinnis Road, where on the south side is the dirt drive and locked gate.

Cabin: This is a classic cabin, built with walls of logs, polished planked floors and red checkered curtains on the windows. It overlooks a small pond that is full of frogs during the summer and makes an excellent skating pond in the winter. Behind it is a cattail marsh where deer are often observed wandering through at dusk.

There is electricity and lights while the kitchen features an electric cooking stove and refrigerator as well as a table, benches and a wood-

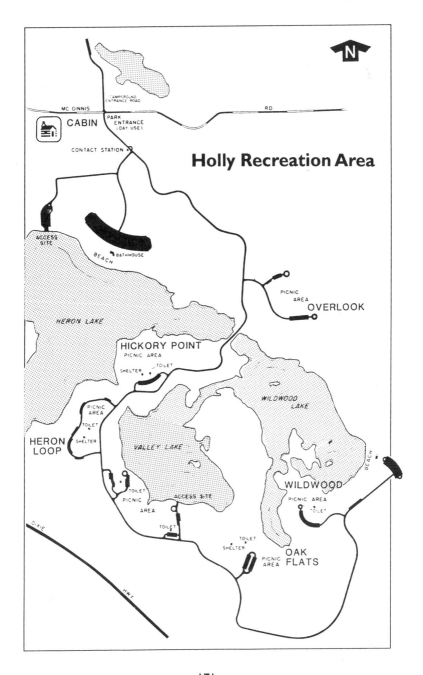

Roston Cabin in Holly Recreation Area.

burning stove. The sleeping room is larger with a set of bunks and easy chair facing a fieldstone fireplace. Overlooking this cozy room is a loft, the warmest part of the cabin at night, with four more mattresses. Outside you'll find a vault toilet, woodshed, a hand pump for water and a grill.

Winter Activities: The favorite activity of winter renters is cross-country skiing. Follow McGinnis Road another quarter mile east to the entrance of Heron Lake day-use area. The scenic road winds 3 miles south around three lakes, Heron, Valley and Wildwood, but isn't plowed much beyond Overlook picnic area at the beginning. At this point the road becomes a perfect ski run, when there is sufficient snow, through a rolling terrain of meadows and woods and past views of the lakes much of the way.

Reservations: Call the park headquarters to reserve the cabin in advance. The most popular season is the winter and is usually booked solid most weekends from late December through February. It's often available in mid-week on short notice, however.

70

SCAUP CABIN
RIFLE RIVER RECREATION AREA

Region: Lake Huron
Nearest Community: Lupton
Bunks: 6
Fee: $30 plus vehicle entry permit
Information: Park headquarter (517) 473-2258

Scaup Lake is one of a handful of new cabins the Department of Natural Resources has constructed throughout the state. Frontier cabins are so popular that Scaup Lake was booked solid on weekends throughout the winter before it was even completed in late November.

If you have every gone winter camping then it's easy to understand why families and others like them so much. It sure beats a pup tent.

During the spring, summer, and fall you can drive to the structure that is tucked away in the south half of the park. But during the winter the roads are not plowed much beyond the headquarters near the entrance. After a heavy snowfall, your choice of transportation to reach Scaup Lake or any of the other four cabins in the park, is limited to snowmobiles, snowshoes. skis or, like the first party that rented it, sled dogs.

Directions: Rifle River Recreation Area is reached by departing I-75 at exit 202 and heading north on M-33 for 20 miles to Rose City. Turn west on Rose City Road and the posted park entrance is reached in five miles.

Cabin: The Scaup Lake unit is built on a small knoll surrounded by paper birch and overlooking the six-acre lake. The one-room cabin is snug and tight, featuring six bunks with mattresses, table, benches, a kitchen counter to prepare meals and a wood burning stove that will keep everybody toasty warm throughout your stay in the woods.

Outside there is a hand pump for water, a wood pile and a vault toilet. Renters need to bring bedding, cookware, lantern, and their own food.

Winter Activities: If there is sufficient snow you can enjoy some great cross country skiing along the park's 12 miles of trails or along its road system. This includes some hair-raising hills ideal for sledding,

The rustic cabin on Scaup Lake in Rifle River Recreation Area.

especially on the trail that skirts Lodge and Devoe Lakes.

Within the park are also 10 lakes and four of them are within easy reach of the cabin and offer excellent ice fishing opportunities. The best is Grebe Lake where anglers rig tip-ups for northern pike, baiting them with small bluegill and pumpkinseed sunfish they catch through the ice.

Reservations: Call the park headquarters to reserve the cabin in advance. Cabins are rented out year round but the most popular season for all of them is winter and by late summer Scaup will be booked solid weekends from mid-December through February.

71

GREBE LAKE
RIFLE RIVER RECREATION AREA

Region: Lake Huron
Nearest Community: Lupton
Bunks: 8
Fee: $30 plus vehicle entry permit
Information: Park headquarter (517) 473-2258

Of the four frontier cabins in Rifle River Recreation Area, Grebe is one of the oldest but undoubtedly the most popular. Its scenic location, excellent fishing opportunities in Grebe Lake and nearby facilities such as fishing docks and observation towers, make this cabin a bargain at $30 a night.

During the winter the roads are not plowed much beyond the headquarters near the entrance. If there is a heavy snowfall, the cabin then becomes a favorite of snowmobilers while others reach it on skis or snowshoes. Like all the cabins in this book, this is an excellent way to spend a winter weekend so plan on booking it well in advance.

Directions: Rifle River Recreation Area is reached by departing I-75 at exit 202 and heading north on M-33 for 20 miles to Rose City. Turn west on Rose City Road and the posted park entrance is reached in five miles.

Cabin: Grebe Lake is tucked away on a small peninsula of its own with the scenic lake spread out all around you. There are some farms at the south end of the lake but two islands in the middle block them out of view for a secluded setting. The one-room cabin is snug and tight and has eight bunks with mattresses, table, benches and a wood burning stove.

Outside there is a hand pump for water, a wood pile and a vault toilet. Renters need to bring bedding, cookware, lantern and their own food.

Fishing: There are 10 lakes within the park but the best by far for anglers is Grebe Lake. The 72-acre lake is a shallow body of water, never reaching a depth much more than 18 to 20 feet. A short walk north along Ridge Road is a pair of fishing piers where children can do well in June and

Ice fishermen jigging for panfish.

July catching pumpkinseed and bluegill, occassionally even landing a few keepers.

During the winter there is generally a few anglers working tip-ups through the ice in an effort to land northern pike. They often bring wax worms and catch small panfish to use as bait and then, with the aid of binoculars, can actually sit inside the warm cabin and watch their rigs out on the ice. How you make it from the cabin, down the snowy slope and across a frozen lake in time to set the hook is something else entirely.

Reservations: Call the park headquarters to reserve the cabin in advance. Grebe, like Scaup Cabin, is booked solid from mid-December through February. Book it in July and August and hope there is snow on the February weekend you reserved.

72

HARRISVILLE CABIN
HARRISVILLE STATE CABIN

Region: Lake Huron
Nearest Community: Harrisville
Bunks: 4
Fee: $30 plus vehicle entry permit
Information: Park headquarter (517) 724-5126

What used to be the contact station for the campground at Harrisville State Park is now one of the newest cabins. The Harrisville Cabin, however, is not in a wooded and secluded location like the rest listed in this guidebook.

It is located on the west side of the campground and during the summer offers a family new to camping a way to ease into the activity. During the winter, however, you would have the campground to yourself, and probably the entire park, as the sites are closed from November through mid-April, making for a comfortable and unusual weekend.

Directions: The park entrance is a half mile south of the town of Harrisville on US-23.

Cabin: This triangle shaped cabin is smaller than most in the state park system but still contains four bunks with mattresses, a wood stove, work counter, and benches. There is no table inside but outside you'll find a picnic table, grill and fire ring. Vault toilets are located within the loop and water is available at the park headquarters during the winter.

Winter Activities: Located right next to the cabin is the trailhead for Cedar Run Nature Trail that makes for a 45-minute walk in the summer and an easy ski in the winter. The trail winds through stands of red pine, wetlands, and across a creek as it swings past the day-use area before returning to the campground at the south end of the loop. A winter afternoon could also be spend wandering the beach to study the ice formations the Lake Huron surf pushes onshore.

Reservations: Call the park headquarters to reserve the cabin in advance. The Harrisville shelter, however, is not nearly as hard to book as many other units are in the state park system.

73

NEBO CABIN
WILDERNESS STATE PARK

Region: The Tip
Nearest Community: Mackinaw City
Bunks: Four
Fee: $25 plus vehicle entry permit
Information: Park headquarters (517) 436-5381

Looking for a snug little log cabin in the middle of the woods? You want to rent Nebo Cabin at Wilderness State Park for a weekend. The small, four-bunk cabin is in the heart of this 7,514-acre state park well away from the campgrounds and beaches along the Straits of Mackinac.

During the summer it can be reached in a vehicle by carefully following a rough two-track road. During the winter, it's a two-mile ski in. And winter, without a doubt is the most popular time to rent Nebo, due to its picturesque setting among towering pines and the fact that it is often half buried in snow.

Directions: Wilderness State Park's main entrance is eight miles west of Mackinaw City and is reached b following County Road 81 and continuing west on Wilderness Park Drive after crossing Carp Lake River.

Cabin: Situated on a small hill, Nebo is a classic log structure. Inside it's one large room with a polished wood floor, beams overhead, four bunks, and a table and chairs made out of split logs. There is also a wood burning stove that doesn't take long to heat the cabin as well as pots, pans and wood cutting tools.

Outside is a vault toilet, hand pump for water, a wood pile and a picnic table. You need to bring sleeping bags, food, water bottles and some source of light, a lantern being the best.

Winter Activities: The ski in is an easy two-mile trip from a plowed parking area off of Wilderness Park Drive. The trail is groomed with a snowmobile but snowmobile activity is not allowed in this area of the park. By continuing south along the trail, you reach a three-sided shelter with its own stone fireplace in another half mile.

Nebo Cabin is a classic log structure in Wilderness State Park that during the winter requires a 2-mile ski to reach it.

Reservations: Like all cabins, winter is the most popular time to rent Nebo. Call the park headquarters six to eight months in advance to reserve on a certain weekend in January or February.

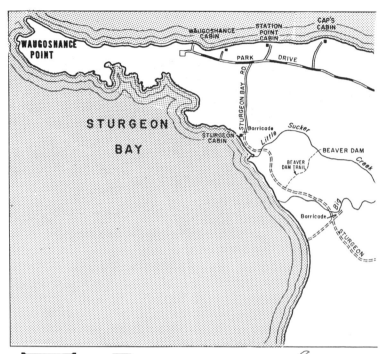

74

STURGEON CABIN
WILDERNESS STATE PARK

Region: The Tip
Nearest Community: Mackinaw City
Bunks: Four
Fee: $25 plus vehicle entry permit
Information: Park headquarters (517) 436-5381

Sturgeon Cabin is a four-bunk unit located along scenic Sturgeon Bay on the west side of Wilderness State Park. Unlike Nebo, this one has quick access to a beautiful beach and an equally impressive view of Lake Michigan, bordered to the north by Waugoshance Point.

But in May and June this cabin is best known as an angler's get-away

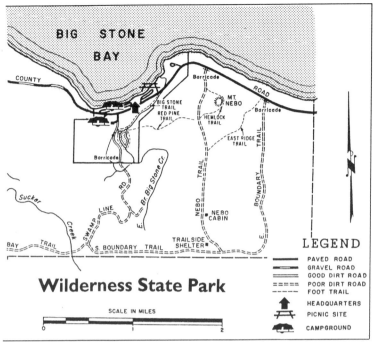

Wilderness State Park

SCALE IN MILES

LEGEND

PAVED ROAD
GRAVEL ROAD
GOOD DIRT ROAD
POOR DIRT ROAD
FOOT TRAIL
HEADQUARTERS
PICNIC SITE
CAMPGROUND

because it is the closest to the rocky points and inlets on the southside of Waugoshance Point. This stretch of shoreline support extensive spawning beds for smallmouth bass, enticing wader-clad fishermen to toss spinners into the pools when the season opens on the last Saturday of April.

Directions: Wilderness State Park's main entrance is eight miles west of Mackinaw City and is reached by following County Road 81 and continuing west on Wilderness Park Drive after crossing Carp Lake River. The park headquarters is off Wilderness Park Drive and here you pick up the key and directions to the cabin within the park.

Cabin: Sturgeon is a stone and log structure situated off Sturgeon Bay Road in the fringe of pine that borders the bay. A few steps through the trees and you break out to the beautiful shoreline found here and can follow it for miles to the south.

Like Nebo, this cabin has four bunks, a table and chairs, a wood burning stove, pots, pans and wood cutting tools. A vault toilet, hand pump for water, a wood pile and a picnic table are outside and you need to bring the same equipment (bedding, food and a source of light) as any other frontier cabin.

During the summer you can drive to Sturgeon Cabin, during the winter it can be reached via a snowmobile. It's only a 3.4-mile run from where the park staff stops plowing the park road but lies along the park's 12-mile snow trail.

Fishing: The most noted fishing opportunity in Wilderness State Park is for smallmouth bass in the north end of Sturgeon Bay when the season opens the last Saturday before Memorial Day. Anglers park at the end of Wilderness Park Drive, put on their waders then hike out a half mile along the south side of Waugoshance Point to toss small spinners and nightcrawlers among the rocky pools and inlets off the shore. From Sturgeon Bay, it would be a hike of about a mile along the shoreline.

Wilderness State Park also has an improved boat launch just west of Lakseshore Campground (see page 60).

Reservations: Plan to call the park headquarters six to eight months in advance to be certain of reserving the cabin on the weekends of your choice and even earlier if you want it on opening weekend of bass season or in May.

LIGHTHOUSE POINT CABIN
CHEBOYGAN STATE PARK

Region: The Tip
Nearest Community: Cheboygan
Bunks: 8
Fee: $25 plus vehicle entry permit
Information: Park headquarters (616) 627-2811

The newest cabin at Cheboygan State Park is also the most popular during the summer, especially when the staff added a screened-in porch. The eight bunk unit is situated only a few yards from a beautiful sandy beach along the Straits of Mackinac in the most remote corner of this 1,000-acre park.

Throw in the fact that there's a gate across the narrow access road

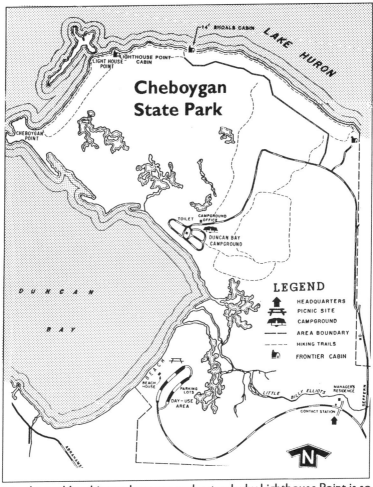

into the park's cabins and you can understand why Lighthouse Point is so popular. It is more than a comfortable escape into the woods. It's renting your own private beach for the weekend.

Others, infatuated with lighthouses, enjoy the sea mariner's touch of the cabin. Within the area you can enjoy six past or present lights, including one from the back porch. During the winter Lighthouse Point becomes a ski or snowmobile adventure as the access road is not plowed.

Directions: The entrance to the state park is three miles east of the city of Cheboygan on US-23. From the park road, the cabin is a 1.6-mile

Lighthouse Point Cabin in Cheboygan State Park.

drive along a narrow dirt road.

Cabin: Lighthouse Point features a table, wood stove chairs and eight bunks inside and a rustic appearance that is enhanced by a peaked roof and square beams overhead and split log siding. Another table is on the porch which faces the water and through the trees you can view the Straits and Bois Blanc Island.

Cabin users need to bring their own bedding, food, cookware and warm slippers. The concrete floor can get cold during the fall or winter. The park provides an ax, saw and logs for the wood burning stove as well as a vault toilet and hand pump for water outside.

Lighthouses: An adventure to Lighthouse Point is enjoying six past or present lights that have been guiding ships through the Straits of Mackinac, the cross roads of the Great Lakes, since the mid-1800s. The first two are seen on the drive in when the access road passes a small clearing. Within the tall grass and overgrown shrubs, you can see the cement foundations and stone walls of the two lights that gave the Point its name. The first was a typical cone lighthouse built in 1851 near the shoreline and soon was undermined by waves. The second was Lighthouse 592, a three-story structure built further back in 1859. It served faithfully until it was taken out of service in the 1930s and finally torn down in 1941.

In front of the cabin is Fourteen Foot Shoals Light, located less than a mile away, while to the east is a view of Poe's Reef Light. Bring binoculars and study the horizon to the northeast and you can spot Martin's Reef Light on a clear day or lace up your hiking boots and follow the shoreline west for less than a mile to Cheboygan Point and search across Duncan Bay for Cheboygan Crib Light.

Hiking: There is a 6-mile network of trails within the park. Skirting in front of the cabin and occasionally marked in red is the 2-mile long *Beach Trail*. To the west the trail extends to Cheboygan Point, to the east it follows the shore, first passing Fourteen Foot Shoals Cabin and then ending at Poe's Reef Cabin.

Reservations: Book the cabin in advance by calling the park headquarters. In the winter, it's best to call between 8-9 a.m. Lighthouse Point is one of the few cabins more popular in the summer than the winter.

Campground Index

CAMPGROUNDS BY REGION
SOUTHEAST

LAKE MICHIGAN

LAKE HURON

HEARTLAND

NORTHWEST

THE TIP

ABOUT THE AUTHOR

Jim DuFresne is an outdoor writer based in Clarkston, Mich. and author of 10 wilderness\travel guidebooks. His books cover areas from Alaska and New Zealand to Michigan's own Isle Royale National Park. His syndicated columns, *Kidventures* and *Travels in Michigan* appear in daily newspapers throughout Michigan.

DuFresne is a journalism graduate from Michigan State University and the former outdoors and sports editor of the Juneau Empire, where in 1980 he became the first Alaskan sportswriter to ever win a national award from Associated Press.

DuFresne's latest title is *Wild Michigan* (Northword Press), a look at the state's wilderness areas. Other recent books include *50 Hikes In Lower Michigan* and *Alaska: Travel Survival Kit* (Lonely Planet).